BECOME
A MILLIONAIRE
IN 21 DAYS

BECOME
A MILLIONAIRE
IN 21 DAYS

SCOT ANDERSON

LifeHouse
BOOKS

Phoenix, Arizona

FIRST EDITION

Published by **Life House Books**
1006 East Benrich Drive
Gilbert, AZ 85295

ISBN 13   978-1-58588-029-4

Millionaire Habits in 21 Days

For more information, contact:

Life House Books at www.lifehousebooks.com

DEDICATION

I dedicate this book to the queens in my life. To my mom, who gave me life and showed me how to live it. To my wife who made life more amazing than I could imagine. To my brand new daughter Savannah whose life brought me so much joy.

TABLE OF CONTENTS

FOREWORD

Great book! Scot Thomas Anderson has hit the nail on the head. Like his dad, Dr. Thomas Anderson, he understands that God gives us the choice to be rich or poor. It's all in how we interpret the scriptures. Obviously, poor people want to believe that God loves poor people more than rich people. Many rich people feel guilty about being rich because so many people think that money is evil. And there are a few who are rich and believe God loves the rich and wants us all to be rich. This is the Anderson family's teachings and why I support their ministry.

Years ago, in Sunday school, I was taught, "The word became flesh." That teaching has guided me for years. As a young boy I began to realize that the difference between a rich person and a poor person was their choice of words, which is why my rich dad forbade his son and me from using the words, "I can't afford it." Rich dad, a very religious man, said, "Poor people use the words, I can't afford it, more than rich people. That is why they are poor."

So if you want to become richer, more prosperous, closer to God, read the words from this great book by Scot Thomas Anderson.

–Robert Kiyosaki

INTRODUCTION

You see things; and you say, 'Why?'
But I dream things that never were;
and I say "Why not?"
—George Shaw

"Scot, you are crazy. You can't become a millionaire in 21 days." Yes, you can, and you will if you apply the "System of Success" I have outlined in this book.

No False Expectations

It is very important that I do not fill you with false expectations. When I say you will be a millionaire, I do not mean in the financial sense. (Please keep reading.) I mean in the mental sense. Twenty-one days from now, you probably will not have a million dollars in the bank, but you will have the tools in you to produce the millions of dollars you desire.

The reason most people can't produce millions of dollars isn't because they don't want to. It is because they go about it wrong. They spend their time trying to get the money rather than changing so the money comes to them. If I can get you to think like a millionaire—become a millionaire on the inside—the money will naturally come.

Well, then, why do I call you a Millionaire?

A person graduates from college with a law degree and we call him a lawyer. But by definition, a lawyer is someone who prosecutes or defends someone in the court of law. That person is called a lawyer, even though he has never set foot in a courtroom as a lawyer and never defended or prosecuted a case. He is called a lawyer because of what is in him. He has the tools needed to be a lawyer. Becoming a lawyer is now a natural process. If he uses the tools, he will find himself fitting into the definition of a lawyer.

A doctor is someone who practices medicine. After years of schooling, he graduates and is called a doctor. Yet, he is not practicing medicine at that time. We call him, "Doctor" based on what he has in him. He knows how to be a doctor. Becoming one is just a matter of time.

That is what we are doing in this book. After reading it, apply the "System of Success" and in 21 days, you graduate as a millionaire. Though you don't have a million dollars in the bank, in you are the tools, information, wisdom, and understanding you need to produce millions of dollars in your life. Now becoming a millionaire is just a matter of time.

You have spent twenty plus years spinning your tires, not going anywhere financially. I am asking you to give me just 21 days. Give me part of a month, to change your entire life. If you give me 21 days, you can become a millionaire!

CHAPTER 1:

Inside Out

*Change has a considerable psychological impact
on the human mind. To the fearful it is threatening
because it means that things may get worse. To
the hopeful it is encouraging because things may
get better. To the confident it is inspiring because
the challenge exists to make things better.*
—King Whitney Jr.

To me, this book is very exciting, because I love change. Whether it is change in my life, or someone else's life, it excites me. Like most of you, I've read hundreds of books on gaining finances and gone to many seminars on becoming wealthy. Sure, a lot of books are just gimmicks. A lot of seminars are just big hoaxes to make those putting on the seminars wealthy. But I did read a lot of good books and went to a lot of great seminars that had great tools for leaning how to invest in land, real estate, stocks and bonds. I, like some of you, spent $500, $1,500, $8,000 on such seminars. After one month, six months, one year, two years, I was in the same financial place I was before. The only difference was I had $500, $1,500, $8,000 less in the bank than I did before the seminars.

I got the principles. I got the tools on how to get wealth, but nothing inside of me changed. I found out how to make money investing, but still inside of me was a force stopping me from stepping out and taking risks. I still had the fear. I still had the stress. I still had the anxiety—and all of this held me back from using the tools I was given.

The tools are important, but if you don't change the inside, you will never be able to elevate yourself on the outside of your life. What is going on outside of you is no more than a reflection of what is in you. You can change all you want outside of you. You can change jobs, change marriages, change addresses, but it seems that nothing changes in your life. That is because what is in you is creating your world. You need to change the inward man, and then the outward man begins to produce.

So you went to seminar after seminar and you got some great tools. You left pumped up and excited. You went home and told your spouse what you were going to do. You told them about the money you would make.

But a few weeks later, it came time to step out. It came time to put some money down, or time to start that company, buy that land. And then what was in you began to come out. You said things like, "Well, the economy is really bad right now. You know, the market is no good. Right now isn't a good time to start a business. I don't know if this invention is that good. Books are hard to get published. You know what? Let's hold off and wait. Maybe next year will be a better time." And one year, two years down the road, you are still in the same financial situation. You're still just getting by in your life.

The sad thing is, during that one or two years of wasting time, over a hundred thousand people became millionaires, using those principles that you said wouldn't work, during an economy you said was horrible, with that same invention you said no one would want, starting the business that you said couldn't make it. Over a hundred thousand people last year became millionaires, and

> **What is going on outside of you is no more than a reflection of what is in you.**

the only difference between them and those that did not is simple. Those that became millionaires thought differently than those that did not. It had nothing to do with their past or their I.Q. It was a simple difference of what was in them. The millionaires were able to step out and take a risk. Those who did not become millionaires had reasons not to take the risks. Those who became millionaires found ways to succeed; those who did not found reasons not to try. Those who are still just getting by had all the reasons why they couldn't, while the wealthy made ways that could. The simple fact is that those who did changed what was in them. Those who didn't stayed the same.

It is time you realize that you will never go beyond what is in you. As you will see, your subconscious will sabotage your circumstances, ideas and life to keep you at the level your mind is at now. It will hold you back. You want more, but your subconscious will not allow you to get more. That's why ninety percent of the people who win the lottery go broke in a short time. Within five years, they are at the exact same place that they were before they won the money. Why is that? If you watch their lives, they are making bad decisions, horrible investments, squandering their money, and sabotaging their lives. Their subconscious is working twenty-four hours a day to get them back to their comfort zone. They may not like being broke, but they feel more comfortable being broke. What is in you will always come out of you.

How many sports stars do we see who make a fortune while they are playing, only to end up selling insurance later in life? Why is it that seventy-five percent of NFL players go bankrupt within the first five years of playing football? They are making millions of dollars only to wind up broke. The reason is, they went beyond what was in them, and their subconscious took them right back to that comfort level.

You will finish this book a millionaire, a millionaire on the inside. In 21 days you will get rid of everything in you that has been limiting your life—those fears, those wrong thoughts, those limiting beliefs—gone. Now you can step out of your old life and step into the life you desire. In 21 days you will change your life from the inside out.

"But changing me won't teach me what to do."

I would say everybody reading this book, deep down inside, knows how to get rich. You know that the only difference between you and the rich person is the way you think. You read about the guy who made twenty million dollars on an Internet idea and, you think, "I had that idea." "I had that invention five years ago." "I looked at buying that land years ago." "I had an idea for that same business."

You knew what to do. That isn't the problem. The problem is stepping out and doing it. The difference between you and the guy who made millions on the invention is one thing: He stepped out and did it. Why didn't you? Because what was in you held you back, while what was in him forced him forward.

Donald Trump is a very smart, gifted man, but inside of you are characteristics and gifts that he doesn't have. Many of you are smarter than

> **Those who became millionaires found ways to succeed; those who did not found reasons not to try.**

he is in certain areas. You are gifted in areas he is not. You have talents he does not possess. Why is he a billionaire, and you are not? Because he thinks differently. Because of the way he thinks, he produces a different world.

You could take all of Trump's money away and in a matter of time he would be a billionaire again. Why? Because of the way he thinks.

> *"You have to think anyway, so why not think BIG!"*
> —Donald Trump

We think small. We think just enough, just get by. Trump thinks big, too much, more than enough. We think of just getting a better job. Trump thinks of getting another multi-billion dollar deal. We look at a business and say, "Too big of a risk to do it." Trump looks at the same business and says, "Too big of risk not to do it."

"Well, it's because of his connections, who he is, and who he knows."

You could take away his identity, you could change his face, take him out of where he is, and I guarantee you, in a matter of time, he would be a billionaire again. You could make him Scot Anderson. It would take a lot of work to make him look this good. We would make him 5'4" (have to cut him off at the knees). Now, you put him in my situation, with my resources, everything I have, and in a short amount of time, he would be a billionaire. Inside of me, I am still changing. Sure, I think like a millionaire, but now I have to take it to the next level and think like a billionaire.

He could become you, with your same gifts and talents. Trump could step into your identity, same money, problems, and circumstances. In a matter of time, he would be a billionaire. Why? Because he thinks differently.

I don't care if you are a single mom. Make Trump a single mom of four, living on welfare. In a matter of time he would be a billionaire. Because of the way he thinks!

This should excite you. This says if you can change how you think, you can change what you have. Get yourself thinking like a millionaire and you will produce millions of dollars.

If you give me 21 days, you will think like a millionaire. Now you can become a millionaire.

CHAPTER 2:

The Power of Belief

"You all have powers you've never dreamed of, you can do things you never thought you could do. There are not limitation in what you can do, except the limitations in your own mind as to what you cannot do. Don't think you cannot. Think you can, and you will!"
—Darwin P. Kingsley

You possess one of the most powerful instruments in the universe! Every single person reading this book needs to realize that he/she has this instrument available right now. This instrument has over twenty billion cells, connected to over twenty thousand other cells. This instrument has the capability of generating over 1,000,000,000,000,000,000,000,000,000,000,000,000, 000,000,000,000,000... (continue those zeros for over eight pages) thoughts, ideas, and insights. They say that the number of ideas you can have are more than all the molecules in the universe. And this is for the least intelligent person reading this book.

I am, of course, talking about your brain. The human mind is the most untapped resource in the universe. The capabilities that your mind possesses, the potential your mind has is so great, you have only scratched less than one percent of it.

Even if you are the least intelligent person, you possess an unbelievable amount of power that is able to—and will—produce millions in your life—IF YOU ALLOW IT TO! If you take the limits off of it. The only thing that can limit your life is you! If you can remove those limits, you step into a world where, "If you can dream it, you can do it!"

"The only way to discover the limits of the possible is to go beyond them into the impossible"
—Arthur Clarke

What has to be exciting is that you have been born into a time of limitless resources and opportunities—as long as you don't listen to the media. The media said last year that the economy was horrible, yet a hundred thousand people became millionaires. Right now, in this time, we live in the wealthiest era the world has ever known. They say there are over two million millionaires, and the number continues to grow. Will you be one of them? The only person who can decide that is you!

"The lack of opportunity is ever the excuse of the weak, vacillating the mind. Opportunities! Every life is full of them...every newspaper article is an opportunity. Every client is an opportunity. Every sermon is an opportunity. Every business transaction is an opportunity."
—Orison Swett Marden

Today you have the opportunity to start down the path of wealth. You have the opportunity to become better at all you do. You have the opportunity to become a better spouse, a better parent, a better friend, a better son/daughter. You have the opportunity to take one step closer to success in all areas of your life.

Your life is full of opportunities. Today, tomorrow, the next day, and the day after

> **The only thing that can limit your life is you!**

that, each day contains twenty-four hours of opportunities. Will you continue to let them pass you by out of your limiting thinking or will you tap into the limitless gifts you have been given and seize the opportunities that will take you to your dreams and desires?

It is time that you realize that you were engineered for success. You were created to be successful. You are one of a kind. There has never been anyone like you and no one will ever be like you again. You have gifts and talents that are second to nobody else in this world. You have unbelievable abilities that are inside of you. If you could take those limits off of yourself, accept that you can, believe that you can, your life would begin to produce.

> *"There is nothing you cannot have once you have mentally accepted the fact that you can have it."*
> —Robert Collier

That's good. There is nothing you can't do. There is nothing that you can't overcome. There is nothing that you can't have, once you have mentally accepted that you can have it, or that you can do it.

Think about this: There are thousands of people out there who are not as smart as you—who are millionaires. There are probably a half a million people out there who are not as gifted as you are—who are millionaires. There are so many people out there who had a worse childhood, had bigger circumstances to overcome than you. They had a worse past than you, yet they have millions in the bank. The only difference between them and you is the way you think. If you begin to think like they do, your life will begin to produce it naturally.

Nearly every study done to date concerning financial success has the same answer. Financial success has nothing to do with a person's I.Q. or with a person's gifts and talents. It has nothing do with their past, with their circumstances. People who are financially successful think differently.

It Is Like a Magnet

You take a piece of iron and magnetize it and that piece of iron can lift twelve times its weight. You demagnetize that iron and it can't even lift a feather. It won't lift anything. It's interesting that in the world today there are two types of people. There are those whose minds have become magnetized. Their minds are full of confidence, magnetized with faith, magnetized with expectation, and they are able to step out and do it. Their minds attract the ideas, the resources and the people they need to be successful. Their minds work just like a magnet. They accomplish more than twelve times what the average person can do.

> **Financial success has nothing to do with a person's I.Q. or with a person's gifts and talents.**

Then you have the other ninety-five percent of the people in the world today. Their minds have been demagnetized by what their parents said or by what the teachers said about them, demagnetized by what the media said, by their own limiting beliefs. They are full of fear, worry, and doubts. Their minds, in a way, push away success. They keep resources, ideas, and people at a safe distance. They just get by. They continue their lives of just average, far below the possibilities of what they should be able to have.

In 21 days, your mind will be magnetized. Your mind will begin to draw everything you need to it. It will attract the people, the resources, the ideas, and the finances you need to accomplish your financial goal.

Deep down inside of you, what you believe is what your mind draws to it. If you believe you can't, guess what? Your mind will draw to it everything you need so you don't.

Whatever you believe with conviction, your mind will move heaven and earth to make true. Your mind will work twenty-four hours a day to produce it.

Let me give you an example of how your mind brings what's in you into your reality. The Super Bowl is coming up, and you have been thinking about a big screen TV for the last nine months. A few months ago, you accepted the fact that you can have a big screen TV. Your spouse, on the other hand, has not accepted this fact. You know that right now the finances aren't where you want them to be, so you tell yourself, "Not now." But your mind begins to work twenty-four hours a day, trying to bring this into your world. It seems like everywhere you turn, you see ads for TVs, articles on TVs. The magnet has been activated. Two weeks before the Super Bowl, you are driving around doing errands when you look up and there is a Circuit City. You think to yourself, "Let's just go in and look around a little." Two hours later you are driving home with your 65" top-of-the-line big screen TV that you financed for the next seventy-two years. Your only problem in life is explaining to your spouse what happened.

I will tell you what happened. You used the power we will use in this book. Your subconscious mind was activated by your faith, beliefs and your expectations.

Your mind then began to draw everything you needed to bring into existence what was placed in it. Using that same principle, we will tap into that same power, and use it to bring the wealth you desire into your life.

Your mind takes you to what you believe. Understand it does not take you to where you want to go, but to where you believe. Your mind will always prove what you believe is true.

> **Whatever you believe with conviction, your mind will move heaven and earth to make true.**

That's why a lot of people want lots of money, but deep down they believe they can't produce it. Because they aren't smart enough, don't have enough talent, or because of their past, it's something they can't have.

If you believe that you can't, your mind continues to prove that you can't. You're a failure because Mom and Dad said, "You are a failure, no good and worthless." So you continue to produce failure into your life. You think you are just average because Daddy said, "Just work a job, and don't try to step out. Don't try to, because the economy is never any good. And you know, wealthy people, they are unhappy. Money causes problems in your life." Maybe some religion told you money was evil. So you have that belief on the inside of you, and your mind says, "I don't want to be evil, so let's not get a lot of money." Or you believe, "We aren't smart enough," so your mind proves to you throughout the day how unintelligent you are.

Your mind will block out anything that contradicts what you believe.

For example, deep down you believe you are a failure. So your mind will not allow you to see the thirty-five successes that you had that day. It can only focus on the two failures.

You believe that you're not smart enough, so anything smart you do, your mind does not show you. It is just the dumb things that you do (we all do these) that your mind lets you see. But the only difference between you and Trump is, Trump focuses on the smart things he does and you focus on the unintelligent things you do.

Your mind blocks out all that is against what your belief system is. What you believe on the inside of you is what is producing in your life throughout the day. If you change your belief system, you begin to change what happens.

What is interesting about this is that it does not matter if what you believe is true or not. If it is true to you, it is true. You may think you are not smart enough. That is totally untrue. But if it is true to you, it becomes your reality. Money is not evil, but if it is evil to you, then all you see in the media and in your neighbor's life is how money destroys.

But compare that with someone like me who sees money as an amazing tool to bless others. I see all the good money does—Bill Gates spending billions of dollars to make the world a better place—I see the money as good.

What you believe will always become your reality!

Let me give you an example:

Take a woman who believes that men are jerks because her dad left when she was young. She was abused by other male relatives. Her whole life, men have always abused her and have always left her. We all probably know a lady like this. It seems like any guy she ever dates or marries is a jerk.

Is she just unlucky? No, it is her belief system. She believes all men are jerks, so her mind will only allow the jerks into her life. You can

> It does not matter if what you beleive is true or not. If it is true to you, it is true.

bring two men into her life. Both men are very handsome, 5'4" tall, sandy brown hair styled out of the eighties. You know the guy (he is on the cover if you need a mental picture.) One man would make an amazing husband. He would love and care for her. He would be true to her, be her prince charming. The other guy is a bum. Life is all about him. He has never been true to any woman. The only time he will come around is when there is nothing else to do. He'll never call her and basically treat her like crap.

I ask you, who will she pick every time? We both know she will pick the jerk. It doesn't matter that the good guy is buying her flowers, chasing her, trying to be the man she needs. Her mindset is, "Why is he all up in my business, smothering me, calling me all the time, getting me flowers and gifts?" (Because, of course, who would want that abuse?) "I just want to be friends with him. He isn't my type." The problem is she has the wrong type in her. She needs to change her type.

You see, she is attracted to the bum who never calls, who is out at the clubs all the time and has nothing to do with her. This is the man she wants. She finally gets him, and a few years of abuse later, he leaves, thus proving to her that all men are jerks. Is that statement true? Absolutely not. But it is true to her, because it is what she believes.

Another example:

You believe that you are unlucky in your investments. You believe that what you try in the financial world fails. It is your belief. So two deals present themselves to you. One is a money-maker and the other is a dog. Which one will you pick every time? You will pick the dog. Thus proving to you that you lack the chromosome needed to make money.

I have a good friend who believes this very thing. For the past decade he has told me how everything he invests in goes to garbage. I watch his life and it is absolutely true. If he buys a stock, it is a guarantee that the company is going bankrupt soon. I actually tell him to let me know what stocks he will be buying so I can sell. I honestly believe he was responsible for each of the stock market crashes in the last fifteen years. I told him he could make a lot of money by just calling companies and telling them that if they don't give him ten thousand dollars, he will purchase their stock. Honestly, anything he invests in fails.

A couple of years ago I had invested in nine properties. I had a great deal on another property drop in my
lap. This friend of mine had seen how much money I was
making and told me he want-
ed in. I was maxed out at the
time, so I presented it to him.
I had everything in place for
him—all he needed was five
thousand dollars down. He
put the money down.

> ...thus proving
> to her
> that all men
> are jerks.

One hour before he was to sign the papers, he called
and said, "I can't do it. Too much stress. I can't handle
it. I want out."

I said to him, "You are going to lose your five thousand dollars, plus what you would make."

He said, "I don't care. I want out."

He got out, lost his money, but also lost over a hundred thousand he would have made on the deal. What
happened? His subconscious would not allow him to get
into a deal that went against his belief system. So it sabo-
taged him. Since then, he has invested in a lot of other
bad investments. He just stays away from the good ones.

There are some of you out there who have had business opportunities, stocks you should have bought, inventions you should have done, things that you should have
been doing, things you knew would make you money. But
your subconscious would not allow you to go against what
you believe on the inside. If you can switch that around to
where you believe that whatever you do is successful, that

you are a money-maker, that wealth is attracted to you, all of a sudden, what you believe becomes your reality.

I believe I have blessing and favor in whatever I do. I believe that whatever I touch seems to turn to gold. In my life, that is exactly what happens. My mind takes me to all the good deals, all the great things. My mind works twenty-four hours a day to bring into existence success.

In 21 days, your mind will be dragging you to success!

CHAPTER 3:

Habits Control Your World

"The beginning of a habit is like an invisible thread, but every time we repeat the act we strengthen the strand, add to it another filament, until it becomes a great cable that binds us irrevocably thought and act."
—Orison Swett Marden

Let's start out with the basics. I believe this will bring a level of understanding that most of you did not have before.

There are two parts to the mind: the conscious and the subconscious. The conscious is the part of the mind that chooses what you will believe. The subconscious then directs the life based upon the beliefs that have been written upon it.

Before we move on, you have to understand how much of your life is controlled by the subconscious. Most psychologists say that ninety-five percent of the decisions you make in a day are subconscious. How you respond to situations, react to your environment, what you think about, most of what you say and do, you do without consciously deciding to do it. It is an automatic response. That means that nearly all of the choices, decisions, feelings and actions that you experience during the day are reactions that you don't think about.

Your spouse says something. You just respond. You have these natural responses that have been put inside of you that just continue to come out your whole life. They've been set in there since you were twelve years old, these natural cruise control responses—ninety-five percent of the time.

That is why a lot of investing books don't work. They have great information, but you only use that information five percent of the time. You read the book, come up with all the things you are going to do, and then five percent of your day you do it, and the other ninety-five percent is spent sabotaging it. You never seem to get anywhere. You say, "I am going to make these new choices and decisions." But that is only five percent of the time. Five percent of the time you are going in the right direction and then the other ninety-five percent of the time your little vehicle turns around and goes the other way. You are never getting any closer to the direction that you want.

What are natural responses? Somebody cuts you off, pulls in front of your car. You have a natural response, right? It just comes right out of you! You didn't have to think about it. You didn't say to yourself, "Okay, now, raise your right hand. Extend your middle finger. Now, with your mouth, say "#$@!" No, it just happens. It's almost like you had no control.

A business opportunity comes up. Right off the bat you say, "Oh, not right now."

You get an invention idea. "No, I can't do that."

A management position opens up. "Not for me. I'm not smart. I'm not intelligent enough." You don't even have to think about it, it just comes right out of your subconscious.

> *"Repeat anything long enough and it will start to become you."*
> —Tom Hopkins

If you change that subconscious reaction or response inside of you from negative to positive, from taking you away from what you want instead of to what you are supposed to be having, if you can change those preprogrammed responses in your life, you will begin to go subconsciously to the life you dream of.

Five percent of your day you do it, and the other ninety-five percent is spent sabotaging it.

Your subconscious mind is like the hard drive of a computer. It's been preprogrammed with things. If you hit the letter "Q" on a computer, a "Q" is going to pop up. You get in there and you double click on AOL, AOL is going to come up. You double click on Word, Word will pop up. Every action has a set reaction in your computer.

Your life is the same thing. A button is pushed in your life; you have a natural reaction to it.

What is interesting about the computer is you can get into the hard drive and mess with the reaction. On a friend's computer we changed it so every time he typed "the," the word "sex" was put into its place. He would finish a letter and "sex" would be in it twenty times. "Bro, you need to get your mind out of the gutter!" we would tell him. Every time he would double click AOL, it would take him to a Gynecologist website.

Inside all of us, we have areas where our "the" doesn't produce what we want. You type in "the," trying to get to success, and it takes you to failure. Your job in this book is to get your actions and reactions to take you to success.

The conscious mind chooses what you believe—what you believe you can do, what you can have, the talents and gifts you possess, your opinions and your views on money, relationships, life in general. The sad thing is that most of these choices were made by the time you were twelve years old. Most of these opinions and beliefs came from what your parents told you, what your teachers, friends, the media and even your enemies said about you or to you. A lot of those things were lies. These beliefs were then written upon your subconscious mind. The subconscious mind then uses this information to direct your life.

Unfortunately, your subconscious mind never argues with the conscious mind. It takes as fact whatever you tell it. If you tell it that you're worthless, it says, "Okay, I am worthless." It then makes decisions based out of that belief. Please remember that its goal is to prove true what you believe. Your subconscious shows you all the worthless things you do and sabotages circumstances in your life to prove to you that you are worthless. Are you worthless? Only if you believe it. Whether you are worthless or successful depends only upon which one you believe.

Your subconscious becomes the cruise control of your life. It makes most of your choices and most of your decisions. Your subconscious is putting forth your attitude, dictating how you respond and react to circumstances in your life. It is creating your world from the inside out.

"Habit is either the best of servants or the worst of masters."
—Nathaniel Emmons

Let me give you an example of the power of the subconscious mind. Remember, much of what you believe was put inside of you by parents, teachers and peers by the time you were twelve. Those beliefs still dictate your life today.

When I was between six months and nine months old, my parents will tell you, I loved fudgesicles, candy bars, and Fudge Pops. Every time Mom would open up the goodies, I would get all excited! For three months they gave me lots of chocolate.

He would finish a letter and "sex" would be in it twenty times. "Bro, you need to get your mind out of the gutter!"

At nine months old, they gave me a fudgesicle, I ate the whole thing, and for whatever reason, I got really sick and threw it up. The next day, when they took out a fudgesicle I wouldn't even put it in my mouth. This made my parents come to the conclusion that I do not like chocolate. (Why? I have no clue, since I had loved chocolate for the last three months.) So, from that moment on, my parents began to say, "Scot does not like chocolate." That is what they began to speak over my life. As long as I can remember, I was told I hated chocolate. At twelve years old, I had a friend ask, "Have you ever tried chocolate?" I thought for a second and said, "Not since I was nine months old."

Isn't it interesting that your parents can put a belief inside of you, and you never try it, you never test it? You just assume it is true and live your life around the belief. You were told, "You're not smart." You never tested that. You were told to just get a job and work your life away. You never tested that. You were told that wealthy people are snobs and look down on people. You never tested that. Your parents said, "You can't succeed." You just took that for fact. Your parents said, "You will never amount to anything," and you just believed it.

The subconscious mind will always prove itself true. So when I tried a piece of chocolate, of course I hated it. Because it is what I believed. "Well, Scot, maybe you really didn't like chocolate." Maybe, but this next part dismisses that theory.

Growing up, I loved ice cream sandwiches. They were my favorite thing. I remember when I was in sixth grade going to Grandpa's house for three weeks. He bought a huge box of fifty ice cream sandwiches. I ate all of those in a week.

I remember Grandpa saying to me, "Boy, you love those things don't you?"

I said, "Yep."

He said, "But don't you hate chocolate?"

I said, "Yes, but what does that have to do with ice cream sandwiches?"

He said, "Those wafers are chocolate."

> **Whether you are worthless or successful depends only upon which one you believe.**

I said, "Grandpa, no, they are not. If they were, I would hate ice cream sandwiches."

He said, "Oh."

And we went on with our lives. I continued to eat all the ice cream sandwiches I could get my hands on.

Then one day I got married. While eating my second ice cream sandwich, my wife asked, "How can you eat that? It's chocolate."

Once again, I said, "No, it is not."

My wife, who, unlike my grandfather, could not be wrong and let me enjoy my true passion, grabbed the box out of the freezer and showed me where it said "chocolate wafers."

All of a sudden the sandwich tasted funny. I told her I liked the ones without the chocolate wafers. I have yet to find those, and I have been looking for the last ten years. And since then I have not been able to eat an ice cream sandwich. That is the power of the subconscious mind. As soon as my mind figured out that was chocolate, "Well, I don't like them, I can't eat that."

Your parents said many things that got down into your subconscious, a lot of which probably is not true. You can't back it up with any fact, but you believe it as true. Even though it is not true, it becomes true to you. And so you continue to make choices based on lies. You continue to miss the chocolate of life, missing the fudge of life, missing the good things of life because of something Mom said when you were seven years old, or something that your teacher said in the first grade.

> *"A belief is not just an idea that you possess,*
> *it is an idea that possesses you."*
> —John Maxwell

Go back to the computer example. We have preprogrammed responses inside of us. These are called habits. These habits dictate what we experience and the life we produce.

Inside of your subconscious are these habits that drive your life. It's the cruise control that takes you places. You have the habit of how you respond to every situation in your life. If you could change the habits, your life would naturally go where you wanted it to go. If you could get the habits of Trump, you would become like Trump. If you could act like a successful person, even ninety-five percent of the time, you would become successful.

> *"The programming that you accept from oth-*
> *ers, and the conscious and unconscious direc-*

tives, pictures, feelings and thoughts that you transmit to yourself, will find a place in your own internal control center. Together, those thoughts and images will continue to create action that will be a part of you and your future."
                                    —Dr. Shad Helmstetter

This book is all about changing the habits inside of you. You will get millionaire habits. It is interesting that you can ask any self-made multimillionaire, "Okay, how did you get that first million?"

And he will say, "You know what? It was a lot of work. I had to work and change a lot of things inside of me. There were a lot of habits and a lot of wrong beliefs that I changed in here that got me that first million. But that second million came really easy. And that third million was even easier."

> **You continue to miss the chocolate of life.**

Why? Because once you change the habits to get the first million, those same habits continue to produce the next million and the next million in your life.

As soon as you change the habits inside, you will see your life begin to change right away.

I have heard it said many times.

> *"We first make our habits and then our habits begin to make us."*
> —John Dryder

If you can get the habits of a successful person, you will become successful. If you can get the habits of a happy person, you will become happy. If you can get the habits of a millionaire, you will become a millionaire.

Most physiologists will agree that it takes 21 days to form a habit. And that's all I am asking of you. If you will just give me 21 days, you can change your life. If you apply the Twelve Laws, in 21 days you will be a millionaire. You will have the habits of a millionaire, and from those habits you will produce millions of dollars.

I challenge you to do all the excersises. Take all the notes in the "Systems of Success" as we begin to go through them, changing these habits. The laws that I am going to give you will drive you to what you want in your life.

You are 21 days from becoming the person who makes your dreams into realities.

CHAPTER 4:

Not My Fault

"Success on any major scale requires you to accept responsibility. In the final analysis, the one quality that all successful people have is the ability to accept responsibility for their lives."
—Michael Korda

Twenty-one days from now, you will be a different person. Your spouse, neighbor, boss, even your own mother will not be able to recognize you. You will have a whole new set of habits, habits that are driving you to the life you desire. From the inside out, you will be attracting all you need for success.

In the following chapters we will go over the "Twelve Laws of Success." Some of the things I ask you to do may sound a little weird. But if I told you that you would become a millionaire if you stood on your fence and crowed like a rooster every morning, would you? Most of you would be right on that fence every morning. It's the same with this.

Some of things I ask you to do, your subconscious mind will resist. Why? Because it goes against your belief system. So it will say things like, "That doesn't apply to us." "That isn't for me." "I don't buy into that." "What does that have to do with finances?" Your subconscious will fight to hold onto its beliefs. But it is these beliefs that have held you back. Don't pick and choose which laws you will apply. Do them all. Just give them 21 days. You give me 21 days, and your whole life will change.

In the following chapters I will be giving you the "Twelve Laws of Success." These are LAWS. Like any other law, they are not dependent upon you believing them. They affect your life whether you believe in them or not. You can say you don't believe in gravity all you want, but it will not change what happens when you jump off the roof.

> *"Progress consists largely of learning to apply laws and truths that have always existed."*
> —John Allan May

The same principle applies to these laws. Whether you decide to believe them or not, they are still true. It does not change the fact that they are affecting your life. You can either get these laws to work for you, or you can continue to fight them. It is your choice. Understand that this is not a buffet, where you pick and choose. If you want your financial dreams, you have to do every law. If you leave out even one, you will not acquire your financial dreams.

Law #1: The Law of Responsibility (In Charge)

"Everyone thinks of changing the world, but no one thinks of changing himself."
—Leo Tolstoy

The Law of Responsibility:
You cannot change what you are not responsible for.

You can't change it if you are not responsible for it. As long as it is someone else's fault, as long as it is your past's fault, as long as it is the economy's fault, your parent's fault, your DNA's fault, you cannot change. There are many millionaires and billionaires out there who had far worse childhoods, worse parents, aren't as smart as you, aren't as gifted as you. The only difference was that they took responsibility for their lives.

"If you don't accept responsibility for your own actions, then you are forever chained to a position of defense."
—Holly Lisle

You see, if you're not responsible for your life, you cannot change it. You are chained to the problems of your life. You are are a prisoner of your circumstances. If you believe you're not responsible, then your subconscious mind says, "Not our problem, nothing we can do about it." So you end up just sitting back and letting life dictate to you what's going to happen.

As soon as you admit that you are responsible for your life, as soon as you say, "I am responsible for where I am today, I am responsible for my financial situation," then your subconscious minds says, "We have some things to fix."

Until you become responsible, you can't go any further. The rest of this book becomes useless to you. Really, why read it if there is nothing you can do about your financial situation anyway? You're just wasting time.

"I never blame myself when I'm not hitting,
I just blame the bat and if it keeps up I change
bats. After all if I know it isn't my fault that I am
not hitting how can I get mad at myself."
—Yogi Berra

Basically if it isn't my fault, if it is the job, the boss, the spouse, the economy, there's no reason to get better, no reason to change. I stay the same, blame everything else, and remain imprisoned to the circumstances of my life.

For some of you, your subconscious is mad about this. It goes against your core beliefs. You are saying things like "Scot, you don't understand my past. You don't understand where I'm at. You don't understand. He left me. He did this. She did ..." or, "You don't understand what my husband did, and he doesn't want to invest. He doesn't want to do anything." You have given yourself excuses to stay where you are. Until you become responsible, nothing will change.

I know a sixty-year old woman who was living out of a double wide just five years ago. Her husband hadn't worked in a decade. Today, she owns her own business, has three rental properties, and is worth over a half a million dollars. What happened?

She will tell you, she stopped blaming her husband (would be nice if he worked), and stopped blaming the economy. She decided that the only person who could change her life was herself.

> **Five years ago she was a single mom living on welfare. Today she is a multimillionaire.**

"Scot, you don't understand. I'm a single mom. What can I do?"

Michelle Hoskins is a person you may have seen on Oprah, or you might have seen her syrup in any Wal-Mart in the nation. I met her last year at a financial summit. She was speaking right after me.

Five years ago she was a single mom living on welfare. Today she is a multimillionaire. What happened? She took responsibility for her life and sold the syrup recipe that was handed down generation to generation all the way back to when her great great great grandmother was a slave. For many years, her finances were not her fault. Once they became her fault, she could change them.

She took charge of her life. I actually like that word better than responsible. Law number one is: Take Charge of Your Life.

"To decide, to be at the level of choice, is to take responsibility for your life and to be in control of your life."
—Abbie M. Dale

You have all of these excuses and reasons why you can't be successful. My goal is for you to create ways to become successful.

That is good enough to say one more time. You have all of these reasons why you can't be successful. My goal is for you to create ways to become successful. The only way to do that is for you to take charge of your life.

I have been playing golf for the last thirty years. Growing up, I had all the reasons why I was terrible at golf. We were poor, so my clubs were the problem. Though they were great in their day, their day was sometime before WWII. I usually played with range balls. So I had the perfect excuse for stinking at golf. Then as I got older, I worked out every day. I must stink because my arms are so tight.

At age thirty-five, it hit me. I hadn't worked out since the day I got married, (sorry, Babe), I had the best clubs, and five-dollar Pro V1 golf balls. Yet I was still horrible. I came to the conclusion that it was my fault. If I wanted to get better, then it was my responsibility. I gave myself a six-month commitment, and for six months I either hit a bucket of balls, or played golf every day. I got lessons every single week. In six months I went from shooting in the mid 90s to low 80s and the occasional 76-79. As long as I had reasons for not being good, I could never take the steps necessary to become good.

The same goes for your life. As long as you have reasons to be broke, you will stay broke. As long as you have reasons to stay depressed, you will remain depressed. As long as you have excuses for why you stay at the weight you are, you will stay at that weight. Once you take charge of your life, your life begins to change.

Are you an "INNY" or an "OUTEY"?

People fall into one of two groups. You will be an external locus of control person or an internal locus of control person.

If you are an external, this means that your life is controlled by things on the outside. Everything that happens to you is from the outside in. So it is the economy's fault. It is the government's fault. It is the union, the job, your parents, your spouse, your past, your DNA or your metabolism. You have no control over life; life controls you. You have to just sit back and take whatever life throws at you.

The rest of the people are internal locus of control, meaning that your life is controlled from the inside out. What is in you produces itself outside of you. My external world is a mirror image of my internal world. I am in charge of my life by controlling me, my thoughts, my attitudes, and my behaviors. If I change in me, I change out of me. If I take control of my thoughts, I take control of my emotions, of my attitude. I can control my world from the inside out. If I don't like something in my life, I have the power to change it.

In life you will find that all successful people are internal locus of control, while the unsuccessful people and the average person who is never going to go past average are external locus of control. You find that all happy people are internal, while all depressed people are external.

Unhappy, unsuccessful people have all their reasons for their bad lives. They have all the excuses. It is never their fault. It is always someone else's. They can't take charge of their lives and change their lives, so they stay in that life.

> *"Character—the willingness to accept responsibility for one's own life—is the source from which self respect springs."*
> —Joan Didion

Laken, my oldest son, was three years old, and he was still dealing a little bit with bed wetting. He got the chicken pox, and my wife has this great rule that when you are sick, you get to sleep in our bed. That way Dad doesn't get any sleep or anything else. In the middle of the night I woke up just soaking wet. At first I thought I was sweating, I felt so hot, and just soaking wet. I went to wipe the sweat off my chest, and just brushed it by my nose enough to notice it was not sweat.

I said "LAKEN!!!"

Laken, half out of it, answered "Yes, Dad." Then he sat up in bed because he realized what he had done.

Just then, my wife rolled over and said "What is going on?"

Laken blurted out, "DAD PEED THE BED!!!!"

We all make those excuses for the beds in our lives, all the reasons why we are not responsible. We all blame everyone else, and in that, nothing ever seems to change.

It is never their fault. It is always someone else's. They can't take charge of their lives.

Look at it this way. You are riding in the car of life. If you are an external locus person, the problem is that you are in the passenger seat. You have no control over where the car is going. If the car is headed towards some trees, you just have to brace yourself. If it's headed towards another cliff, just hold on. There is nothing you can do except scream and just hope to luck out for a change.

I would hate an existence where I have no control over my life whatsoever. Finances bad? Sorry, nothing you can do. Marriage bad? Sorry, nothing you can do. Sorry, you have depression? Nothing you can do.

I love my life as an internal locus of control person. I am in the driver's seat of life. Yes, there may be some speed bumps in life, and maybe a tree is in my way, or a cliff up ahead. But I have a sense of control over my life. I can grab the wheel and get around that tree. I can turn the whole vehicle around if I have to. I can put the brakes on or speed up. Yes, there will be problems. Yes, there will be rocky roads up ahead, but at least I have control over where my life ends up.

As soon as you take responsibility for your life, as soon as you climb over into the driver's seat, your life immediately begins to change. It may take a while to get on a better road, but at least you have a sense of control over how you experience the ride.

It is about time that you say, "I have the ability to obtain wealth. I have the gifts, the talents needed to make my financial dreams a reality. You know, there are millionaires out there who are not as smart as me, as gifted as I am. I am turning this car around, and I am headed towards my dreams, aspirations, and my goals in life. I have no one to blame. Instead I take charge of my life."

In 21 days, you will be in the driver seat of life, headed towards your dreams and desires.

System of Success (S.O.S.)
Exercises

Exercise 1:

The goal is for your subconscious to take responsibility for your life, for you to take charge of your life. For the next 21 days, throughout the day, I want you to repeat to yourself, **"I am responsible for my life. I am responsible for my life."** I will discuss with you in great detail the power of this later in the book. For now, take my word for it. Say it over and over again, until your subconscious believes it.

Exercise 2:

List excuses you have had in the past for why your life is the way it is. Under each, write out how you can take responsibility for that area in your life and change it. I understand that if you say, "Because of the rape when I was ten," there is nothing you can do to change that. But you can say, "I can't change the past, but I am in charge of my future. I will not allow my past to hold me back in my future."

Excuse:

My responsibility:

Excuse:

My responsibility:

Excuse:

My responsibility:

Excuse:

My responsibility:

Exercise 3:

For the next 21 days, anytime you have a problem in your life, write it down. Include things that make you upset or annoyed. This includes arguments with your spouse, friend, family member or boss. Now write down under each problem what you could have done differently. This helps you see that you do have control. Sure, you may fight daily with your spouse. You may feel like you have no control. This exercise helps you see that you do have control. Maybe if you responded differently to your spouse, if you said things with a different tone, if you thought ahead, the fight might have never happened.

Problem:

What I could have done differently:

Problem:

What I could have done differently:

Problem:

What I could have done differently:

Problem:

What I could have done differently:

Problem:

What I could have done differently:

Problem:

What I could have done differently:

Problem:

What I could have done differently:

Problem:

What I could have done differently:

Problem:

What I could have done differently:

Problem:

What I could have done differently:

Problem:

What I could have done differently:

Problem:

What I could have done differently:

Problem:

What I could have done differently:

Problem:

What I could have done differently:

Problem:

What I could have done differently:

Exercise 4:

List the three biggest problems in your life. Then under each problem list three or more things YOU can do to help fix the problem. Once again, you are headed toward a tree in the car of life. Grab the wheel and do what you can do to change the direction.

Problem:

1.

2.

3.

Problem:

1.

2.

3.

Problem:

1.

2.

3.

Problem:

1.

2.

3.

CHAPTER 5:

Why Be a Passenger When You Can Drive?

This life is yours. Take the power to choose what you want to do and do it well. Take the power to love what you want in life and love it honestly. Take the power to walk in the forest and be a part of nature. Take the power to control your own life. No one else can do it for you. Take the power to make your life happy.
—Susan Polis Schutz

Law #2: I Like Being in Control

The Law of Control:
   I feel happy to the degree to which I am in control.

The level you feel that you are in control dictates your level of happiness.

Have you ever been in the passenger seat, riding with a really bad driver? They are swerving in and out of traffic, looking way too much at you while they are driving, right on the back side of the car in front of you. Remember in the movie Dumb and Dumber when Loyd was driving the hot girl to the airport. He was actually completely turned around talking to her while cars were crashing all around him.

My mom was such a driver. I cannot honestly tell you how many stop signs we drove through because she did not see them (I always told her we would stop twice on the way back), or how many red lights we sped through. It wasn't because she breaks the law, but because she had other things on her mind. Later in the book we will talk about confessing things over your life. Usually while driving, she had her confession book out, reading as she drove.

I was excited that Mom was changing from the inside out, but other cars were coming from the outside in! Going for a ride with Mom while growing up was anything but relaxing. "Mom, red light. MOM, red light. MOM RED LIGHT!!!!!"

"What dear?" she would say.

"Never mind, Mom, love you."

While you are in the passenger seat, you are stressed out, not happy, not relaxed. This goes for life. When you are not in control of your life, you are not happy. You are stressed out, full of fear, worry, anxiety.

When life is out of control and you are a victim to circumstances, it is impossible for you to be happy. When you feel like you have to go to work, you have to do what the boss says, and you have to go home to a marriage that feels like a trap, you have no control over your life whatsoever. The only time I have control is when I sit down in front of the TV. Now I can control what I watch. That is why so many people spend over four hours a day watching TV. It is the only time of the day they have any sense of peace, because it is the only time of the day they feel like they are in control.

> *"People who learn to control inner experience will be able to determine the quality of their lives, which is as close as any of us can come to being happy."*
> —Mihaly Csikszentmihalyi

Let me ask you this: Is there anything in your life that you have to do?

"Well of course, Scot. I have to go to work."

Do you? Does someone show up in the morning with a rifle, tie you up, gag you and take you down to work? Honestly, do you have to go to work? Of course not. There are a lot of things you can do. You have the freedom right now not to go to work again. You can quit, go to dance school, go back to college, become a lawyer, start a business, become an astronaut, a bum, a cook, a dentist, a doctor. Right now you can do anything you want to. You are in control. You are in charge.

The problem is most people don't realize this. So they spend their whole life feeling like they have to.

"I'm trapped in this marriage." No, you're not. There are a lot of things you can do. Now, they may not all give you the results you want. But you are not trapped. You have control. I'm not saying that all of these are the best options. But they are options. You can leave. That is an option. You don't have to stay with your spouse. You can get counseling. You can become a great husband/wife. You can read books, listen to CD series on marriage, go to marriage seminars. You can get separated. You are in control of where this marriage goes. You are not trapped.

But as long as this marriage is something you have to do, you won't have any happiness in it. It is not until you get to be married that marriage is the greatest thing to happen to you.

A lot of men feel that they have to go home to their wife. I get to go home to my best friend. They have to spend time with her. I get to spend time with her. They have to do things together. I get to build a life with her. There are a lot of things they don't get to do because they are married, I have a lot of things I get to do because I am married. They are miserable. I am the luckiest man on earth. They have no control. I am in control.

For some of you, this chapter is going to be like a pressure valve that just got released. You will feel like a heavy weight was taken off your shoulders.

You don't have to do anything. My goal in this chapter is to get you from having to do things to getting to do things. There is a big difference. There is a huge difference between having to work and getting to go to work. This changes your attitude, how you respond in the day, your creativity, your production and, most importantly, how happy you are. One way I have no control; the other way I am in control.

A few weeks ago I tried an experiment on my son. Sorry, Laken, my little twelve-year-old guinea pig. My goal was for this summer to be the summer of golf for him. I want him to become good at golf.

So week one, I went to him and said, "This week, if you want, I will drop you off at the golf course in the morning. You can go play a round of golf. You can practice on the range. When it gets too hot, go into the clubhouse. You can get all the snacks you want, check out all the cool clubs and stuff. I will pay for a lesson any day you want one. When you're done, you can call and we will pick you up."

It is not until you get to be married that marriage is the greatest thing to happen to you.

He was so excited. Every day that week he would get up early, ready to go when I was leaving. He would come home telling me about all he had done that day.

Week two, I went to him and told him I was proud of how hard he had been working the week before. Now I spun how I said the rest to him. I said, "This week we are going to get serious about golf." Every morning he was going to the golf course, he was going to hit some balls, practice his game, he would get lessons twice this week, and I expected him to play a round of golf every day.

Now realize that this is exactly what he had done the week before. This is exactly what brought him so much joy the week before. But now I had to drag him out of bed. He kept making up reasons why he shouldn't go. He whined and complained the whole time. He usually tried to get my wife to pick him up after just an hour at the course.

What was the difference? Week one he was in control; week two he lost control. How many people drag themselves to work, look for reasons to get out of work, try to go home early, hate their jobs? Why is that? Because they feel like they have to. They have no control. But if we can switch that to, "I get to," switch it to, "I have control," now you are excelling in whatever is put in front of you. You are happy. You are becoming more successful every single day.

In 21 days, your life is going to be a life of get tos, no longer have tos.

Now you get up in the morning and you get to go to work. There are millions and billions of people all over the world who would give anything to work in America, to have the opportunity you have to go to work and earn even our minimum wage. My brother recently did a huge concert in Cambodia. The hotel manager, he said, was the hardest worker he had ever met in his life. She worked six days a week, oftentimes eighteen-hour days, never less than twelve hours. She made forty dollars a week. When he talked to her, she thought she was the luckiest person because she got to work. Most people there have no job.

So when you get to go to work, you are excited about your day. Your mind is clear. It's creative. It is able to solve problems. You have an air of confidence. You say, "I don't have to be here. I can find another job, start a business. I am here because I want to be here." You come into the office with a great attitude. The boss sees you differently, and treats you differently. Co-workers do the same. You are in control of your day and your life. You quickly move up the corporate ladder. You start making twice as much money and you use that money to invest, to start a business. Before long you get to run your own company.

> **In 21 days, your life is going to be a life of get tos, no longer have tos.**

In the marriage, you are in control. You know that you can't change your spouse, but you can change yourself. You can become the best husband/wife in the world. You make a life of romance and fun. You can love your spouse unconditionally because you get to. You control your marriage by controlling yourself.

What is interesting in life is that there is only one thing you can control. You can't control the economy. You can't control your spouse. You can't control your boss. The only thing in life that you can control is you. Isn't it time that we started controlling the one thing we have control over?

> *"The first step toward success is taken when you refuse to be a captive of the environment in which you first find yourself."*
> —Mark Caine

In 21 days you will be so happy about the life you are getting to live. Excited about controlling the car of life, making it take you to all your dreams and desires.

System of Success (S.O.S.)
Exercises:

List the things in your life that you feel you have no control over. Now list the options you have. Next write out what you plan to do in each area.

Now rewrite what you felt like you had no control over into a "get to" statement. For example: Instead of "I have to go to work," it becomes, "I get to go to work." Now you can say, "I get to be married." Until you believe this, say it over and over throughout the day, or anytime you feel like you have to. Our goal is to reprogram our subconscious.

I feel like I have no control over:

What options do I have?

What do I plan to do?

Rewrite the statement into a "get to" statement: Then confess this statement over and over.

I feel like I have no control over:

What options do I have?

What do I plan to do?

Rewrite statement into a "get to" statement: Then confess
this statement over and over.

I feel like I have no control over:

What options do I have?

What do I plan to do?

Rewrite statement into a "get to" statement: Then confess
this statement over and over.

I feel like I have no control over:

What options do I have?

What do I plan to do?

Rewrite statement into a "get to" statement: Then confess this statement over and over.

I feel like I have no control over:

What options do I have?

What do I plan to do?

Rewrite statement into a "get to" statement: Then confess this statement over and over.

I feel like I have no control over:

What options do I have?

What do I plan to do?

Rewrite statement into a "get to" statement: Then confess this statement over and over.

CHAPTER 6:

Cause and Effect, Sow and Reap, Action and Reaction

"You cannot hold on to anything good. You must be continually giving—and getting. You cannot hold on to your seed. You must sow it—and reap anew. You cannot hold on to riches. You must use them and get other riches in return."
—Robert Collier

Law #3: Cause and Effect

The Law of Cause and Effect:
What goes around comes around.

If you go to church, then you know it as the law of sowing and reaping. If you are a scientist, then it is, "Every action has an equal and opposite reaction."

If you do something, then from your action there will be a reaction in your life. If you respond to your wife in a moody tone, there's a good chance you will reap a plentiful harvest of moodiness back. If you are rude to the lady at Circle K, chances are, she will be rude back. If you plant tomatoes, you will get tomatoes. If you sow negative thoughts, then you will feel negative. If you sow fearful thoughts, you will have fear in your life. Whatever you sow, you will reap.

> *"Shallow men believe in luck. Strong men believe in cause and effect."*
> —Ralph Waldo Emerson

Your world is being created by what you plant. What you planted yesterday is what you're getting today. If you want a different crop tomorrow, then you have to plant different things today.

The biggest thing I want you to get out of this is that every thought is a seed. Wealthy people realize this. The rest of us don't. We just let our thoughts go wherever they want to go, not realizing that there is a price to pay for every bad thought, every negative thought, fearful thought, each thought of your bad past. Every thought will produce itself in your life.

Every thought that you have is a seed that is planted into your subconscious. That thought then triggers a picture. That picture produces an emotion. That emotion creates an attitude. That attitude creates an action. That action produces a reaction in your life.

If you don't like the reactions you are getting, you have to go to the source, to the seed, to the thought. If you want to change your life, you first have to change your thoughts. As a man thinks, so is he. Your life is no more than the harvest from the thoughts you have planted.

"You become what you think about most of the time."

—Tyrone Edwards

What do you think about most of the time? All the negative in your life? The bad things that have happened to you? Why you can't get a break? Fearful thoughts, stressful thoughts, depressing thoughts? Then you wonder why you are stressed out, full

> **Your world is being created by what you plant.**

of fear, depressed. You cannot plant weeds and expect to get corn. You cannot plant negative thoughts and then wonder why you are depressed.

You inner world is giving you a picture of your outer world; your outer world is just a mirror image of what's inside. If you change in there, then you begin to change what's out here.

One more time. Thoughts trigger ideas, trigger a picture in your mind, trigger an emotion, then an attitude, then an action and finally a consequence.

"Good thoughts and actions can never produce bad results; bad thoughts and actions can never produce good results."

—James Allen

The reason why so many people can never change anything in their lives is they are trying to change the effect rather than going to the cause. You change jobs, change locations, change spouses, change friends, change everything outside of you, but nothing ever changes. If you will go inside of yourself and change the cause, you will see the effect change rather quickly.

"Only when you make the right changes to your thinking do other things begin to turn out right."
—John Maxwell

When we moved into our current house, we had a massive tree. About a month after we moved in, the tree got some rare tree disease and died within three days. We cut the tree down.

I noticed that there was a large drip hose that watered the tree. Since there's no reason to water a stump, I handled the problem the Anderson way and wedged a golf tee into the hose. A few months later I pulled into the driveway to see this hose squirting water madly all over the place. The hose was just whipping in the wind. There was water everywhere. I got another golf tee, shoved it in and fixed the problem.

A few months later, the same thing happened. The pressure had blown the tee out. I did this for the next three years. Five or six times a year, I had to fix this thing. Finally I got some intelligence and decided to follow the hose and see if I could plug it up differently. I followed that thing all the way back and found out it was the only hose on that line. No wonder it had so much water pressure. I went to the sprinkler control box and turned that line off. I never had another problem.

I was dealing with the effect, month after month. Finally, one day I went to the cause, and within a minute, fixed it for a lifetime.

It's the same for your life. You keep fixing the same effects, day after day. You keep having blowups, and emotional meltdowns. You are stressed out, full of fear and worry. If you will just go to the cause, the effect gets fixed very easily.

What we don't understand is that thoughts control ninety-nine percent of our lives. Your thoughts have the ability to raise or lower your blood pressure and to raise your heart beat. Thoughts affect your digestive system (anyone who had to give a speech for the first time knows what I'm talking about). Thoughts can actually change the chemical composition of your blood. Thoughts affect your sleep. Thoughts can make you happy or sad in an instant. (Watch *Titanic*. I'm laughing one moment, then crying the next.) Thoughts can make you feel:

Confident or Inferior
Peaceful or Stressed Out
Powerful or Powerless
Excited or Upset
Happy or Depressed
Calm or Angry
Popular or Rejected

Your thoughts have the ability to create your entire world. What you sow is what you're going to get.

> *"Make every thought, every fact, that comes into your mind, pay you a profit. Make it work and produce for you. Think of things not as they are but as they might be. Don't merely dream—create!"*
> —Maxwell Maltz

I love that. Make them pay you. Put them to work. Your thoughts have been terrible employees up until this time. Now make them work for you. Take charge of your thoughts (Law #1). Become responsible for your thoughts.

Say to your thoughts, "Guess what, thoughts, you work for me now. You are going to put in a good sixteen-hour, hard working day. I am sick of your laziness. I am sick of your negativity. You are going to produce good stuff today."

You make them pay you a profit. Make them work and produce for you.

In 21 days your thoughts will be positive, hard-working employees, who are dragging you to your dreams and desires.

The System of Success (S.O.S.) exercises will be with Chapter 8.

If you have time, I encourage you to read chapters 7 and 8 before putting the book down. All three chapters, 6 though 8, really go together.

CHAPTER 7:

Control Your Thoughts and You Control Your World

"The programming that you accept from others, and the conscious and unconscious directives, pictures, feelings and thoughts that you transmit to yourself, will find a place in your own internal control center. Together, those thoughts and images will continue to create in advance, or influence on the spot every response, attitude, and action that will be a part of you and your future."
—Dr. Shad Helmstetter

Law # 4: Control Your World

The Law of In Control:
I can control my world by controlling my thoughts.

Law number four might be my favorite, and also one of the most important laws. Law four is the Law of In Control. Yes, we have a Law of Control. This one is the Law of In Control.

Law four states that I can control my world by controlling my thoughts. Since thoughts control my world, when I can control my thoughts, I control my world.

*"Of course we become what we think about.
The real question is, do we know what we are
thinking about?"*
—Steve Siebold

One hundred percent of happy people say, "I have control of my thoughts." One hundred percent of depressed people say, "I do not have control over my thoughts." This goes back to the law of responsibility. As long as you cannot control your thoughts, you will have no happiness. As soon as you get in that driver's seat, you have the ability to be happy, to be successful.

Right now think about a beautiful sunset. Now think about a dragon. Now think about a nun whose outfit is dyed pink, with clown shoes on, and a big rubber nose. See, you have the ability to tell your mind what to think. You can control your thoughts. The problem is that most people just let their thoughts go wherever they want.

*"Successful people control their thoughts.
All others let their thoughts control them!"*
—Scot Thomas Anderson

This is a great story about horseback riding. My dad, who was raised in the back woods with no electricity or indoor plumbing, grew up on a horse. He may have been born on one. I don't know. He is like the horse whisperer of his day. He can make a horse dance.

I, a city kid, was around a horse for the first time when I was twelve years old. My dad decided to take the family horseback riding. I was so excited. I had visions of being like the Lone Ranger, or Heath Barkley from the *Big Valley*—a lone cowboy on his trusted steed. The anticipation was nearly killing me. Finally, out came my steed. From a distance the horse had no steed-like qualities. He seemed to limp and his head was barely off the ground. The horse's back looked like a hanging noodle. As the horse got closer, things did not get better. I'm not sure, but I think the horse was used in the Civil War, probably one of the oldest horses in the world.

> **One hundred percent of happy people say, "I have control of my thoughts."**

They got me up on my mighty stallion, and off we went. Not where I wanted to go, wherever the horse wanted to go. Everyone else took off ahead and I was stuck over by a tree. Father Time chewed grass, went to the bathroom, and I think he even took a nap. I tried all the tricks of the trade I had picked up from the *Big Valley* and *The Lone Ranger*. I said, "Giddy up," did that "ch-ch" sound. I took the reigns and swatted them ahead and said, "Giddy-up," while gently kicking my heels into the horse's side (being careful not to kick them through the horse). Nothing. That stupid horse sat there, crapping and eating.

Finally, my dad rode his horse back and said, "Son, what are doing?"

I said, "I think I'm horseback riding, not sure. The horse won't move. I think he is ready to die. I can't see his face, maybe he's already dead."

My dad said "Grab those reigns!"

I said, "I have them."

"No! I mean grab them with some authority! Yank those reigns in the direction you want that horse to go. Give that horse a big kick in the side. Show that horse who is boss!!!"

So I yanked those reigns and kicked that horse. The horse got mad, reared up a little, tried to fight me back. I yanked those reigns again, the horse got mad but started to go in the direction I yanked him. Once in a while that horse would test me, and try and go a different direction. I would yank those reigns again, and he would go where I wanted. After about ten minutes, getting the horse to do what I wanted was effortless. I just pulled the reigns a little to the right, and we would go right. I pulled a little to the left and we'd go left.

The same thing is going to happen to some of you reading this book. Your thoughts have been running your life. They've been sitting out in the pasture eating grass and crapping on your life. You thought there was nothing you could do about it.

Starting today, you will grab those reigns and yank those thoughts to where they should be. Yes, they will fight you in the beginning. They will rear up on you. But just yank those things back to where they belong. When you start to have a negative thought, you grab those reigns and yank them to a positive thought. When you start thinking you're not smart enough, you yank that back to, "I am very smart." When you think you can't, you yank it back to, "I can do anything I set my mind on."

You used to wake up in the morning saying, "I'm tired and I'm down and it is going to be a bad day and this is going to go wrong and I may fail at this and I may fail at that." You have all of these bad things going on through your mind. Instead you say, "NO! It's going to be a GREAT day! It is going to be a successful day! I'm taking another step towards what

> **Your thoughts have been...sitting out in the pasture eating grass and crapping on your life.**

I want in my life." You yank on those thoughts and tell them where to go. Grab them by the reigns. Because for the next 21 days, every thought you have WILL PAY YOU A PROFIT!

What is going to happen is in 21 days, having good thoughts is going be effortless. Just a little tug on the reigns. Get up in the morning, tug those reigns right into, "What a great day this will be. I have so many gifts and talents, and so many opportunities in my life."

Every day, throughout the day you are telling your thoughts where to go. By controlling your thoughts, you control your emotions, your attitude, your actions, and of course, most importantly, your consequences in life.

"Our subconscious minds have no sense of humor, play no jokes and cannot tell the difference between reality and an imagined thought or image. What we continually think about eventually will manifest in our lives. Unfortunately most of us are completely unaware of this fact and we do not monitor our thoughts with the care needed so that we can create in our lives the results we say we want. Since the great majority of people do not feel worthy and deserving of abundant good fortune, radiant good health and total success in all areas of their lives that overriding thought pattern controls the results people get. The first order of business of anyone who wants to enjoy success in all areas of his her life is to take charge of the internal dialogue they have and only think, say and behavior in a manner consistent with the results they truly desire."

—Sidney Madwed

Warning: I want you to see that letting in even one wrong thought is like touching a hot stove. You just want to touch that negative thought, just want a quick pity party, a quick "Poor me." You just want to think about your bad past for a moment. Even though you just touched it, like touching a hot stove, it leaves an emotional blister that lasts for weeks.

Give me just 21 days where you don't touch even one bad thought. Now your life seems to just go towards your dreams and desires.

The System of Success (S.O.S.) exercises will be with Chapter 8. I suggest you don't stop here, instead read Chapter 8 before you put the book down. It is a short chapter, but it and Chapter 7 need to be read at the same time.

CHAPTER 8:

Substitute a Great Life for What You Have

"It's never to late to have a wonderful childhood."
—Larry Wilson

Law #5: The Law of Substitution

The Law of Substitution:
Your mind can only think one thought at a time.

Right now, at the exact same time, think about being on the beach in Hawaii and sitting in only your underwear in a blizzard in Iceland. You cannot think both at the same time. But when you are in Hawaii, you have the ability to substitute Iceland and instantly change what you are thinking. You cannot think good and bad at the same time. What would happen in your life if every time you had a bad thought, a limiting thought, an "I can't" thought, you replaced it with the right thought?

The Law of Substitution says you cannot think of unhappy thoughts and happy thoughts at the same time.

You can't think negative and positive. If you're struggling with this habit of thinking the wrong thoughts, then you simply apply the Law of Substitution.

> *"Keep your mind off the things you don't want*
> *by keeping it on the things you do want."*
> —W. Clement Stone

It's very simple. If you begin to think down about yourself, make yourself begin to think up. If you begin to think on the negative, make yourself begin to think on the positive. If you think unhappy thoughts, simply replace them with happy thoughts. Whatever it is, you supply it.

If your mind keeps going to a particular problem and is keeping you up at night, switch your thinking from, "It's a problem" to "It's an opportunity." If you failed over here and you're thinking about the failure, instead, do what Ford said:

> *"Every failure is just an opportunity to start*
> *over with more intelligence."*
> —Henry Ford

I love that. It is a totally different way of thinking than we have been trained. Every failure is just more of a chance to start over with more intelligence. You have learned from your mistake. You have more wisdom, more experience, and you can now start over more intelligently.

I have had plenty of businesses fail. Was I a failure? No. Were they failures in my mind? No, they were lessons.

For five thousand dollars, I learned a lot more than I ever learned in any seminar. In a lot of ways it was well worth the money.

You substitute every bad thought with a good thought. Substitute "I'm not smart" with "I am very intelligent." Substitute "I can't" with "I can do anything I put my mind to." Substitute "I'm a failure" with "I'm a success in progress." "I hate life...I love life." "I am depressed...I am so happy."

> **You have more wisdom, more experience, and you can now start over more intelligently.**

I want you to make a commitment that for just 21 days you will only let good thoughts in. For 21 days you will substitute all bad thoughts, all negative thoughts, and all "I'm less than" thoughts with positive thoughts.

For 21 days you will only let good thoughts come in, only positive, because your good thoughts are the fuel that will take you where you want to go.

In your car, you would never think about mixing gas with water. "Well, I'll throw a little water in it." No, because your car will sputter and not get you where you want to go. Many of you are mixing. "Well, I can have just one negative thought. No one realizes how bad of a childhood I had, what a bad life I have." You throw a bunch of water in the gas tank and then wonder why you aren't going towards your hopes and dreams.

Remember the hot stove? You can't even touch a negative thought. It will leave a mark for weeks.

"Scot, you don't realize my circumstances." That thinking is what has held you back. It goes against Law One: "In Charge." You are saying you are not responsible. Your circumstances are responsible for your life. I am saying your circumstances are not from your past. They are not because some outside force is against you. It is because of what is happening in you. Your thoughts for years have been running wild and producing these problems in your life. Take responsibility for your thoughts, and in 21 days, you will see the circumstances change in your life.

If you get anything out of this chapter, let it be that circumstances have no control over your happiness. It is the attitude you assign to the circumstance that does. I have a lot of problems in my life, in many cases more than a lot of you. Wealthy people, for the most part, have more problems than poor people. The poor person is responsible for his/her life and maybe his/her family. I have a hundred employees, nine businesses, and millions and millions of dollars out there. In a given day I have a lot of problems. Problems do not dictate my mood. I do. Problems do not decide whether I have a good day or not. I do. If I allowed circumstances to dictate my life, I would not have a good life. Sure, today I will have some problems come up, maybe some big ones. But no matter what happens, today will be a great day.

"It is the way we react to circumstances that determines our feelings."

—Dale Carnegie

Let me give an example. A few weeks ago my mom, on her television show, talked about how I am always positive. Every day is a great day no matter what happens. Here is my day that inspired her thinking. It was a Saturday morning at about 6 a.m., three hours earlier than I like to see my children. The kids ran in, "Daddy, Daddy, we have a swimming pool."

"Yes, kids, I know. Now let Daddy go back to sleep," I said.

> If you get anything out of this chapter, let it be that circumstances have no control over your happiness.

"No, Dad, we have a new pool in the basement!" they exclaimed.

I looked at my just-as-confused wife and said, "Did you put a pool in the basement?"

"Nope," she said.

We ran downstairs to find six inches of water. The insane dog was jumping in and out, then running soaking wet throughout the house. I waded through water toward the bathroom only to see a little brown trout (a turd) floating by. The toilet had been plugged, and then kept running for a day. My two big screens, my Xbox 360, Play Station II, my eight other game systems, DVD players, a computer, (I was working on it and had taken it off the counter and put it on the floor) surround sound…all my other electronics were in the water.

I went to check the circuit breakers, good thing they had blown. I then went back down and shut off the water and got on the phone. I got a company to come out. It took four hours of hard work to move everything out of our new water park. While going from upstairs to down, it seemed really hot upstairs. I kept turning down the air, and it kept getting hotter. Finally, I noticed that one of the AC units was not working. I called an AC guy and he came over. The motor went out.

The pool guy knocked on the door and said something about the main pump being out and it will cost five hundred dollars to fix. "Fine, go ahead."

I got the mail only to see that the local police department had so generously taken a snapshot of me while driving and sent it along with a ticket.

In the same mail was a ten thousand dollar bill that was very unexpected. Though this sounds like too much for any one person to handle, I assure you this is a true story. I also got a notice from the IRS that I made mistakes on my 2004 taxes and owed them lots of money. What makes this funnier is that my records were in my walk-in safe, which is in, yes, the basement. Though it is fireproof, it is not water proof, and all of such records were now very wet.

Later that day my business partner called me about a business I thought was doing well. It happened that a guy working for us stole a ton of money. This was my day.

My mom called me late that afternoon. My wife had given her a rundown of my day. She was calling to just be there for me.

I answered my phone with my energetic, "How is the best Mom in the world?"

She said, "Good," and then with a sympathetic voice, said very solemnly, "How are you doing?"

I, of course, as always, answered very excitedly, "I'm doing awesome."

She said, "Really??? How is your day?"

I said, "Great!"

She then paused for a moment and said, "I thought..." And then she went through all the things that happened. She finished with, "Sounds like you are having a bad day."

I said, "Yes, I guess it sounds like a pretty bad day, but I'm out with the family. We have a great night planned, which includes a pool party in the basement. Overall, today was a great day!"

> *"Every day that I have is a great day! Circumstances do not tell me what my day is like. I tell my day what it is going to be like."*
> —Scot Thomas Anderson

The basement can take care of itself. The ticket? No big deal. Six thousand dollars? Whatever. Those things do not bother me. I can focus on, "I have an amazing wife. I have great kids. I have a house. I have opportunities. I have an amazing future." I can worry and be stressed out (of course that would never change the circumstances) about what is going wrong, or I can be excited about all the things that are going right. I focus on the good, and guess what? Every day of my life is a great day.

At times I do have to come down a little bit. I was at my grandparent's funeral. They had both died in a horrific accident where Grandpa had a heart attack and Grandma got trapped in a burning car. People would say, "Scot, how are you?" The look on their faces when I said, "I'm doing great," told me I couldn't say that. It was a habit. I have a habit of always having a great day.

Sure, that was a very emotionally hard day, but in a way, it was a great day. They lived a great life and are in a better place. Family and friends I had not seen in twenty years got to together to remember all these two amazing people had done in their long lives. Circumstances do not dictate my day.

"I tell my day where it is going, and it always gets there."

—Scot Thomas Anderson

This will be you in 21 days. When you get up in the morning, grab those reins! "Well, what about this and that?" It doesn't matter about this and that. Today is a great day because you are taking one more step toward your success.

Give me 21 days of no negative thoughts, 21 days of only positive thoughts allowed in, 21 days of only saying, "This is a great day." All of a sudden, negative thoughts are a thing of the past. You'll never have any more negative thoughts. All you do is live where Scottie lives—in the land of amazing days, right by the river of peace, the mountains of opportunities, overlooking the valley of joy.

In 21 days, every day will be an amazing day full of opportunity, great experiences, happiness, joy, peace, and love. Every day you know you are one step closer to your dreams and desires.

System of Success (S.O.S)
Exercises

Write down your most dominant negative thoughts. Next to each negative thought, write down a positive replacement thought.

For example:

Negative Thought	My New Replacement Tought
I'm not smart enough.	I am smart enough to do anything I put my mind to.
I can't.	I can.
Too much pain in my past.	I have learned so much from the past.
What a bad day.	What an amazing day.

Negative Thought	My New Replacement Tought

I, _____, commit myself to the following:

For the next 21 days, every time I have one of these negative thoughts, I will replace it with my new thought.

I will not allow any negative thoughts to wander through my brain for the next 21 days. I will grab those reins and yank those thoughts where I want them to go.

CHAPTER 9:

Who is Holding Me Back?
Oh Yeah, It's Me

*This is the true joy in life, being used for a purpose
recognized by yourself as a mighty one. Being a force of
nature instead of a feverish, selfish little clod of ailments
and grievances complaining that the world will not devote
itself to making you happy. I am of the opinion that my
life belongs to the whole community and as I live it is my
privilege—my *privilege* to do for it whatever I can.
I want to be thoroughly used up when I die, for the harder
I work the more I love. I rejoice in life for its own sake.
Life is no brief candle to me; it is a sort of splendid torch
which I've got a hold of for the moment and I want to
make it burn as brightly as possible before handing it on
to future generations.*

—George Bernard Shaw

In this chapter, we are going to get into some psychol-
ogy and some teaching you might have thought was very
deep, but which will be clear and simple to you now. I
believe this chapter will literally change your life. It is the
main reason I went from just getting by to abundance in my
life. It is the reason my mom went from not being able to

read at age twenty-four to authoring four worldwide best-selling books. My dad grew up in a line shack with no electricity or running water until he was in high school. He had to work nearly a hundred hours a week to just keep a roof over our heads and food on the table. However, in just the last seven years, he went from just getting by to being a multi-millionaire. This chapter, if you will allow it, will literally transform and change your entire life.

Law #6: The Law of You

The Law of You:

> *How you see you determines the*
> *level of life you experience.*

Whatever level you are at in life is determined by how you see yourself. Your life will never go too far beyond the picture of yourself you hold inside of you.

How you see yourself affects more than just you. How you see yourself also determines how the world sees you and how the world experiences you. If you don't like how you are treated, stop trying to change everyone around you. Start by making the change in you.

Under the Law of You, your life is limited by how you see yourself. The sad thing is your life should be limitless, but as I said earlier, the only thing that has the power to limit you is you. You have a limitless life, yet how much you make is determined by how you view yourself. Your relationships, marriage and children all work the same way.

They are determined by and limited under the Law of You. If you want a better life, it starts with YOU!

> *"Trust yourself. Create the kind of self that you will be happy to live with all your life. Make the most of yourself by fanning the tiny, inner sparks of possibility into flames of achievement."*
>
> —Foster C. McClellan

Self-Concept

In this chapter we will talk about what psychologists call self-concept. It is interesting to note that most physiologists say that the greatest discovery of the twentieth century is the self-concept.

Psychologists tell us that your self-concept, in a nut shell, is the idea that each person develops a bundle of beliefs at birth regarding him or herself.

You are not born with a self-concept. Instead, it is formed from all the ideas, the values, the virtues and the opinions in your life. It is these things that direct your life.

If you want a better life, it starts with YOU!

If you believe that money is evil because some religious church put that belief in your heart when you were growing up, you will say, "Well, if money is evil, I don't want to be evil." So your subconscious works very hard to keep money away from you.

If your parents told you that you weren't smart and teachers backed that up in the classroom, then now, deep down, you have the belief that you are not that smart. That belief affects your entire life every single day. The decision of whether or not you will start a business or go on to college, who you feel you are worthy to be around, what you can do, what you say, how you experience all of life, came out of one single lie!

As I discussed in earlier chapters, the subconscious is your hard drive, like the hard drive on a computer. It is where all of your beliefs are stored. The conscience mind pushes a "Q" on the keyboard. A successful person has a "Q" come up. A lot of us push a "Q" and we get a "Z". For some of us, a setback comes and we know we should grow from it, push through it, solve the problems, but instead we give up. We get down on ourselves. We have a pity party. We didn't get the outcome we know we should have.

If the subconscious is the hard drive, your self-concept would be the operating system. It is like the Windows of your mind.

Think about what happens to your computer if you have a problem in your Microsoft Word program. I guess you will have to use Works or some other typing program to get your letter done. Not the end of the world. You can still get on the Internet, still work with pictures and still play games.

But what happens if Windows goes down? Well, nothing works. You can't open Word, Excel, get on the Internet. You have no games, no computer. Windows is the hub to the computer, and if it ain't working, nothing is.

It's the same with your self-concept. If your self-concept isn't working, it does not matter what you do. Nothing will work in your life. You can go to all the seminars and they can give you all the ideas you need to invest, but because you self-concept has a virus and isn't working, you continue to fail. Trump could come and drop a company in your lap that has been running for the last ten years, and it's just a matter of time before you sabotage it and bring it down because of your self-concept.

In 21 days, we are going to get that operating system working the way it is supposed to so that instead of working against you, it is working for you. It is

> **If the subconscious is the hard drive, your self-concept would be the operating system.**

making all the programs in you work faster, better and a lot more efficiently. My life changed when I upgraded to the Scot 5.0. The same will happen in your life.

For your whole life, your self-concept has been pulling you down. In 21 days, it will pull you up. It will drag you, push you, pull you to your hopes and dreams. It will put you on its back and carry you if it has to.

Let me give you an example of how a wrong self-concept can sabotage your life, how it can pull you down to its level when you go beyond it. This may have happened to many of you in other forms or ways. Or maybe it happened to your parents.

Let's assume that, while you were growing up, you were told that you are not book smart, but you have a strong back like your dad and your granddad. You heard, "We work with our backs, work hard, and we put food on the table." You grew up hearing about how horrible managers were, how lazy they were and how badly they treated hard workers. One day, at sixty-five, if you save, you can retire and live on social security.

Now that belief is embedded in your self-concept. You have been working for the company for fifteen years. After all those years of hard work, and because you have been basically doing a manager's job anyway, the company takes notice of you. For the last five years, without the title of manager, you ran the crew, made good decisions on the fly and worked great under pressure. So they promote you. They make you a manager.

But this goes beyond your self-concept. Your self-concept says that because you are not smart, you are not management material. Your self-concept also tells you that managers are bad people. This is your belief, and subconsciously, you don't want to be a bad person.

You have just gone beyond your self-concept. The moment they offer you the position, your stomach goes into a huge knot. You can't catch your breath. The stress is near the breaking point. Over and over you say in your mind, "I can't do this." Fear and anxiety take hold of you. You can't sleep. You can't eat. It doesn't matter that they have doubled your salary. This is not worth it.

Your subconscious immediately goes to work. It has to bring you back down to your comfort level. It has to sabotage you so it can get you where you feel safe and secure. It has to pull you down.

At the office, decisions you used to make on the fly, you can't make anymore. You hesitate. You second guess. And it seems like you always guess wrong. The fear holds you back from doing what you know should be done. You have never been late for work, but now it seems like everything works against you, and you find yourself late. Workers who were your friends start talking bad about you. All of this continues until finally, the company says that they have to take the position away and put

> **Your self-concept says that because you are not smart, you are not management material.**

you back to where you were before. You may not like the pay cut, but you go home and you say, "I feel really good about this, I'm not management material." It feels like the world was lifted off of your shoulders.

You conclude that you just weren't cut out for management. The truth is you weren't cut in—in you. You had the ability, the gifts, the talents. Maybe you needed to read some books on management, but basically you were the person for the job. You had already been doing the job, but your self-concept pulled you down. It kept you from doubling your salary and putting you into a place where you could invest that extra $30,000, and in a few years have your own company with your money working for you, rather than working so hard for your money. That self-concept pulled you down.

I want my self-concept to be so high, it has to work twenty-four hours a day at pulling me up to it. Instead of sabotaging my life, it creates my life.

> *"Trust yourself. Create the kind of self that you will be happy to live with all your life. Make the most of yourself by fanning the tiny, inner sparks of possibility into flames of achievement."*
> —Foster C. McClellan

Another example is a man who has a fairly low self-image. From past break ups, and what his parents have said, deep down he doesn't think he is that good of a catch. He meets and starts dating his dream girl. She is so far out of his league (not true, but that is his belief). She is too good for his self-concept to keep.

He begins to sabotage the relationship. His fear of loss makes him so possessive, so jealous, that he becomes a nut. And before long, she leaves. He might not like it, but deep down, it is a relief.

When the Concept Was Developed

Your self-concept was formed between the time you were born until about the age of twelve.

(As a side note, I think that one of the saddest things is that by the age of twelve, you have developed ninety percent of your self concept. I knew nothing about life at age twelve, yet my life was determined by the beliefs I had already formed.)

Those around you while you were growing up helped shape this self-concept of yours. If you had positive parents and they were putting positive ideas in you, then for the most part, you probably have a positive self-concept. If they were putting negative ideas in you, then you probably have a negative self-concept.

But you can even have great parents like I do, amazing parents, and still have huge limiters in your self-concept.

My parents told me I could do anything and be anything, but words are not enough. We learn so much more from their example.

Your self-concept was formed between the time you were born until about the age of twelve.

When I grew up, we were very poor. I try to explain to my kids that a trip to McDonald's was a huge event. Even then, we didn't get a happy meal. I got a hamburger, a water, and the family split an order of French fries. I wore $2 Yellow Front shoes, the ones with the big rubber thing on the front. (Of course they actually just came into style. I guess I was thirty years ahead of my time.) My entire school wardrobe cost less than $15. At Christmas, we got just a few little things. One year I actually got a garbage can. My Green Bay Packers garbage can was one of the best gifts ever. We didn't have much, just our imaginations, so my brother and I used the can for so much. We played basketball with it, hockey, football toss, marble madness. It was a building for our matchbox cars. We even used it to play rodeo with the cat. We put the cat under it and then released and roped her up.

My dad was very smart and a hard worker. Every company he worked for went from a two-employee company to 100 employees. He gave the companies multi-million dollar inventions that are still used today. He worked six days a week—for barely any money.

Though my parents said, "Go and be," what I saw was, "Go and work for The Man." The example I was given was: get a job, don't invest, just work hard. My parents always said things like, "Money is not important." Isn't that what poor people say?

But actually money is very important. I do believe that I can be happy with or without money, but it is a whole lot easier with money. The number one reason for divorce today is money. The number one reason for poverty is money (that statement is kind of funny). Most of the problems in the world could be helped greatly with money. Think of the good you can do for the world with money, the time you could give to the community, to the church if you didn't have to spend all your time working for money. Money is very important. But if you believe it isn't, your subconscious says, "Okay. No big deal. We don't need it."

My parents said, "Go to college and find something you love to do." This is the statement of most middle class parents. It's not what wealthy parents tell their kids. I think it puts a wrong concept into the children's minds. Wealthy parents say, "No, kids. Build a business so your money works for you and now you can do what you love to do."

Some may say, "Okay, start a business doing something you love." That's okay if you can, but I say do a business that makes lots of money, and then start a business doing what you love to do.

I believe you can be happy doing any job. We will talk about that later. I was happy flipping Whoppers (one of my all time favorite jobs), or loading concrete, bussing tables, picking up trash, cleaning buildings, scrubbing toilets.

I know a lot of people who went to college to do what they love. They got themselves an art degree, and are miserable today just getting by. I realize that there are many things more important than money, but in that statement, we give an excuse to people to settle for a life without it.

> **When kids go to college they learn much about dedication, about working hard, about life.**

I think college is important, I don't want to give the wrong idea. When kids go to college they learn much about dedication, about working hard, about life. Now let's make some money. Let's build a business. Let's get that money working for us. Then go and do what you love to do.

> *"Perhaps the most valuable result of all education is the ability to make yourself do the thing you have to do, when it ought to be done, whether you like it or not; it is the first lesson that ought to be learned; and however early a man's training begins, it is probably the last lesson that he learns thoroughly."*
> —Thomas H. Huxley

My uncle got his degree in geology. He worked a job he hated for twenty-some years. He worked hard. He made $70,000 a year and lived on $30,000. He invested the rest.

He retired at the age of forty-five, moved to his dream place, and now donates his time, teaching at a public school and working for his church. He did what he had to do, so now he can do what he wants to do.

Most of us were taught, "Do what you want," and then we got stuck doing what he have to. You got the teaching job because you wanted summers off, but because our system is all messed up, you don't make enough to live on, so you are doing construction all summer long to make ends meet.

I'm not saying you shouldn't be a teacher. I'm saying that while you are a teacher, start a business. Get money working for you. See the importance of money, because with it, you can give so much more back to life.

My parents said, "Do what you love to do." So I decided to be a P.E. teacher. I wanted to blow a whistle all day long and have the summers off. Is there something wrong with doing that? No, but it would have limited my life had that been all I did. I believe you can be a great teacher and make lots of money in a business. But that wasn't in me. What I had in me was, "Money is not important. Just get by."

Just seven years ago, my parents began to see a dramatic change in their life. Seven years ago they were still just getting by. But my mom and my dad began to change some things they had in their self-concept, things that they were thinking. In just a few years, they became millionaires. This should excite some of you. Those of you who say, "I'm too old," should reconsider what you believe. Once again, a limiting belief is sabotaging your life.

It is never too late to change your self-concept. Get that wrong thinking out and get the right things in.

"Well, Scot, you don't know my past. You don't know all the hurts and the pains."

> *"People who get into trouble in our company are those who carry around the anchor of the past."*
> —Jack Welch

My mom had one of the worst childhoods that you could possibly imagine. At nine months old, she was beaten black and blue until she was barely recognizable, because Grandma wouldn't come out of the locked bedroom to get her beating. It was not just physical, but some of the worst emotional abuse you can imagine. She moved from home to home because no one wanted her.

What I had in me was, "Money is not important. Just get by."

She ended up with Great Grandma who consistently told her she was dumb, that nobody liked her, and that she would amount to nothing.

That is what she grew up with. At age twenty-four, she couldn't even read, and when she got married, she couldn't drive. She was quiet, withdrawn, could never speak up in a crowd.

Today she has her own TV show with millions of viewers. She speaks all over the world, is a best-selling author, and a multi-millionaire from all her investments. With that type of past, how is this possible? She did what I am teaching you in this book. She changed her self-concept. She changed down deep in her self-concept. She changed that operating system in her, and because she has done that, her whole life has changed. Her past had no effect on her future. The same can be true for you.

> *"Do not sacrifice your future on the ALTAR of your past."*
> —Scot Thomas Anderson

Mom changed that voice in her head. You know the voice. It's like you can barely even hear it, yet it speaks to you throughout the day. It whispers to you all day long. It is that subconscious of yours whispering out of your self-concept, out of what you believe about yourself.

It is guiding you into all the choices and decisions that are dictating your life. It is speaking to you, telling you where to go and what to do.

It's saying things like, "We can't do that. You're not smart enough. Let's just give up. This is a waste of time. You're fat. You're ugly. Look at that nose of yours. Look at all the problems in your life. Why doesn't anything go right for you? You will never find the right person. You will never have money. You will never get ahead. Don't start that business. Too risky. Don't invest. Don't write that book. You're tired. Just relax. Don't work on that thing that will actually bring money into your life. That problem is too big. Life is depressing. I'm so miserable. Remember…" (Then it takes you back to the hurts of the past).

It continues to whisper things throughout the day. It continues to guide and direct where you are going in your life.

Her past had no effect on her future. The same can be true for you.

I want your self-concept to be where mine is. My self-concept gets mad at anything limiting, anything negative. It says, "What do you mean you can't? Yes, we can. There is nothing we can't do."

An employee comes and says, "There is no solution to that problem."

"Well, then, we don't have a problem. Get out of my office and don't come back until you have a solution. I guarantee there is one. And you don't want me to have to find it, because I do not need problem finders. Those are easy to hire. I need problem solvers."

My self-concept says there is nothing that we can't do, nothing we can't overcome. Get yours to that place and all of a sudden, instead of hindering and pulling you back, it begins to coach you and speak to you and push you and drive you to the success that you really want into your life.

In 21 days your self-concept will not be dragging you back, but it will be pushing you forward. Pushing you to your dreams and desires.

CHAPTER 10:

The Real You!

I do not want to die... until I have faithfully made the most of my talent and cultivated the seed that was placed in me until the last small twig has grown.
—Kathe Kollwitz,

There are three parts to your self-concept. Number one is your self-ideal, that is, the ideal image of yourself. As we go through this chapter, remember that phrase—your ideal self.

In essence, it is what you desire to be. Deep down, what is the ideal you? Who are you as a spouse, as a parent, as a friend, as a business person? It is your vision of yourself.

We all know what we want to be. You have a picture of yourself in your mind of what you think of as the ideal you.

Listen closely to this next part. Successful people have a very clear perception of their ideal self. They have a very clear, concise and specific vision of themselves. The average person does not. The average person has a cloudy, fuzzy idea of who he/she wants to be.

"One of the hallmarks of the great ones is their level of awareness as to what they are willing to fight for. They're willing to suffer and sacrifice to make their visions reality."
—Steve Siebold

In Proverbs it says, "Where there is no vision, success will fail." Where there is no vision, finances will fail. This means when you don't have a clear vision of what you want, you can guarantee that you will not get it.

"People will never attain what they cannot see themselves doing"
—Karen Ford

You have to have a very specific vision. Unfortunately, ninety-five percent of the people living today do not have a clear vision of who they want to be. There vision is generalized and not specific. Deep down, they really don't know.

To say that my ideal vision is, "To be rich," is not very specific. How do you prepare for that? Where is that? What is rich? For some, having ten grand in the bank is rich.

For you to say, "I want to be a good husband," is like saying, "I want to go somewhere warm." Where in the world is the land of good husband? How do you become something when you don't even know what it is?

Successful people have a very clear self-idea. Now listen to this. The greater the clarity or the clearer the vision, the faster you will move toward it.

You haven't been moving toward your ideal self because you have no idea of where your ideal self is.

"You've got to be very careful, if you don't know where you are going, because you might not get there."
—Yogi Berra

Three years ago, I thought I loved myself and everything was great in my life, but I didn't have a clear vision of exactly who I wanted to become in the future. It wasn't until I did the exercise that is at the end of this chapter that I realized I was not moving toward anything in my life.

The greater the clarity or the clearer the vision, the faster you will move toward it.

You are going to write a vision of who you want to be, the ideal you. You're going to finish you. I love that. You are going to finish yourself.

You need to know that you can't be successful at anything unless you finish it before you start it. Let me say that again. You have to finish before you start. If I want to build a house, I have to finish the house before I start to build it.

I have a very detailed set of plans that tells me where every outlet belongs, where every wire is going to go, where every pipe fits, where every toilet in the house is going to be. I have to finish the house first. Then I can start it.

If you were to build a house like most people try to build their lives, just grab a hammer and some nails and here you go, it would be a mess—like most people's lives.

"What kind of house you building, Scot?"

"A nice one."

What is that? How big is that? How many bedrooms? Bathrooms?

Off I go to build my house. I pour the concrete, only to find out I needed to put down some plumbing first. Now I have to tear up the concrete. So many people keep starting something, then tearing it down. I want to do this, and then that. I finally get the concrete in and my wife says, "No, I want the toilet over here." Tear it up again. I put a wall up. "No," she says. "Not big enough."

If that was how you built your house, you would spend your whole life just tearing it up and you would never finish it.

Most people today do that with their lives. They are over here and they want to go there and then they want to go somewhere else, and they are never able to get anywhere because they don't have a clear vision of who they want to be in their lives.

"If you don't know where you are going, any road will take you there."
—Lewis Carroll

We are going to finish you and then we are going to start.

Imagine what kind of vacation I would have if I said, "Holly, get all the kids, all seventeen of them." (I don't know how many we have anymore. I lost count.)

We get them all lined up and take a roll count and Holly asks, "Where are we going to go?"

"I don't know. I thought somewhere nice."

> They are never able to get anywhere because they don't have a clear vision.

Where's nice? To some, Alaska might be nice, for others, Hawaii. Some hate Hawaii and think San Diego is nice. How can she pack, prepare, and get ready for vacation when the vision I have is "somewhere nice."

How do I get there? Do we just start driving and see where we end up? Where do I turn? What direction do I go? How do I prepare?

Very obviously, you can't do that. You have to finish the vacation first. You then can start it. You have to be specific.

"We are going to San Diego. These are the dates we are going. Here is the hotel we are going to be staying at and, Holly, this is what we are going to be doing."

Now we are able to prepare for the vacation. We have all that we need to have a successful vacation. We probably don't need a snowboard and we probably don't need heavy jackets. But we will need a swimsuit; my little thong style Speedo will be fine. Once we finish the trip, we then can prepare for it, and then we can move toward it.

And what is so amazing and awesome about a vision inside of you is that it is the most powerful thing you can get into your subconscious. Proverbs says that a vision brings boundaries into your life. Once it's in your subconscious, your mind begins to move heaven and earth to get you there.

"Vision, it reaches beyond the thing that is, into the conception of what can be. Imagination gives you the picture. Vision gives you the drive and impulse to make the picture a reality."
—Robert Collier

Now we have a clear vision of the vacation. We are going to San Diego and now I have parameters. I have something in me pushing me to it. I will work eight hours packing, shopping, getting the car ready and packed for this vacation. Eight hours and ninety-two suitcases later (only one duffle bag is mine), we are ready.

Only a vision could get a man to do that. Only a vision would get me in a car for six hours, listening to five kids and Barney the Stupid Dinosaur who loves you and loves me—as he sings a song that I know will be the song played in hell for eternity. While driving, I am not guessing which way to go. I know because I know where we are going. Sure, there might be a detour or two on the way, but I know the end destination.

If you can get these same principles working in your life, you will see yourself putting time you never knew you had into doing what you would have never guessed needed to be done, moving you toward a goal you did not know existed.

Vision might very well be the most powerful force in the universe. What gets a person to get up in the morning and run thirteen miles a day? Vision to run a marathon. What gets a gymnast to work out six hours a day? A vision. What got me to lose twenty-five pounds in a week, even though

> **Vision might very well be the most powerful force in the universe.**

my body fat was already below three percent? What got me to not eat for seven days, not drink liquid for two days, run seven miles a day while wearing sweats? (Stupidity might be a good guess.) I wanted to wrestle at 105 pounds. It was vision. Vision will drive you, push you, and drag you to that which you finished in your heart. We have all seen vision work in our lives, yet we never really grasped that this power is readily available to us.

For example, for many of us, there came a time when we got a vision for our first house. We went out and loved it. They said, "Okay, we will build it, and in six months, we need $10,000 down."

In the last thirty-three years of your life, you managed to save $18.33, and now you are asked to save $10,000 in six months? How in the world is this possible?

VISION! Vision won't let you buy things you do not need—that dress, that DVD. Vision forces you to do things you have never been able to do. Vision gets you to work a second job that you never had time to work before. You found ways of saving that you told yourself before were not there. You gave up things you would have never given up. And six months later, you have exactly $10,036 in the bank. That vision brought parameters into your life. That force drove you to what you finished in your heart.

What would have happened if the builder said, "In six months we need some money from you."?

"How much?"

He says, "Don't know. We just need some money."

You would never have gotten even close to $10,000. Remember, I said earlier, if you can dream it, you can do it. The only thing holding you back is you. Some of you will have a $10,000 ideal self written out. I challenge you though, don't sell yourself short. Why become a millionaire when you can be a billionaire? Whatever you finish, your subconscious will take you to.

It will force you to invest, make you step out and take some risks. It will drive you to read books, listen to CDs and go to seminars. It will force you to become that ideal you.

At the end of the chapter, you will be asked, what do you want to be? What is the ideal you?

You may say, "I want people to like me."

Once again, where in the world is that? That is like saying, "I want a nice car." Your subconscious has no idea where that is, so it just keeps you where you are.

Instead of that, begin to be specific. If I want people to like me, what does that mean? It probably means that I need to be a patient person. I need to be a compassionate person. I probably need to get over my fears. I need to love people. Specifically, I have to have a genuine love for people. I have to be able to listen. I have to have a good sense of humor. I have to be able to get people to open up. I have to be trustworthy. I have to be lovable.

I begin to list all of these specific things. Now I have a destination. My subconscious can now begin moving toward that. I can now prepare for the journey. I know what books to read, what things to work on. If I find myself going in the wrong direction, my subconscious says, "Hold on, you were not a good listener back there. You were actually rude. Turn the car around. Let's fix that."

Why become a millionaire when you can be a billionaire?

You say, "I want to be a good husband." Where in the world is that located? I believe that nearly all married men want to be good husbands, yet most are not. Why is that? Because men have no idea where the land of good husband exists. You can't prepare, because you have no idea where you are going.

Instead of, "I want to be a good husband," list what you need in order to become a good husband.

"If I am going to be a good husband, I am going to need to be a good communicator. I better learn to listen, not just to what she is saying, but more importantly, to what she is not saying. I must learn to hear what she needs. I better learn how to communicate what is going on in my world in such a way that it makes her feel loved. I have to learn how to always put her needs first. I have to treat her like a queen. I have to realize that she is the most valuable thing I have. Every day I am willing to lay my life down for her. I have to learn how she receives love, so that what I do is making her feel loved. I better find out what is important to her, and give it to her. When I get home, I must spend the first part of my night giving into her. No TV, no computer. Instead, I sit and share my day with her for the first thirty minutes. I better take her out for a special date every week, and I better become a romantic person. Flowers should be on the table every week. Even though they are a waste of money, my wife loves to brag about me and show her girlfriends, "Yeah, we have flowers on the table every week." "He is so romantic," all her friends say. I better take her on a couple of trips every year, away from the kids and the business. Rekindle that fire. She better become the queen of my world."

Now you have something to work toward. You know how to prepare for that. It is a very clear ideal self.

All of a sudden, when I have created the ideal me, I am a great husband. My subconscious mind is able to do that. We need to take our wives out on a date. We need to be romantic. How do we prepare to do that? The subconscious mind says "I can do that." That vision drives you to be a great husband.

You want to be a wealthy person? That's the biggest thing in here. "Well, I want to have lots of money."

Once again, where is that? Your subconscious has known that for years, yet it never takes you there. That is because it does not know where there is. Clarify the vision.

"If I want to be wealthy, then I better be a problem solver, and sometimes be able to be one in the midst of a crisis. I have to be calm and level headed at all times. I can't allow circumstances to dictate my moods. I can't allow my emotions to be all over the place. I have to become a good decision maker. I can't be full of fear, stress or worry.

> **To be wealthy, I will have to become a risk taker.**

"I better have good thoughts. I have to have a lot of wisdom in the industry I am going to go into. To be wealthy, I will have to become a risk taker. I have to surround myself with people who are going in the same direction I am. I can't stay with friends who want to hold me back, who want to judge me and put me down. I cannot be around negative people anymore. I need positive people in my life. I better start becoming a better manager of my time, because I know that wealthy people say time is their most valuable asset. I can't waste time or let it pass me by. I have to have self-control. I can't just waste my money. Every dollar wasted is an investment I cannot make."

Do you see the difference? Your subconscious mind says, "Okay, this is how we prepare. We had better get good at managing time. We better get good with problem solving. And we better get some books and tapes. That vision forces you to read two books a week. You stop listening to radio in the car. Instead, you now listen to self-help CDs on investment.

Your vision gets you to step out and start that business you have been talking about for fifteen years. Before long, you find yourself wealthy.

Most books out there say, "Get a vision for your life." That doesn't work. I want you to get a vision for who you want to become.

Having a vision for lots of money never works. But if you get a vision to become a person who produces lots of money, that always works.

When you get a vision for who you are going to become, then life will naturally just flow out of you. The difference is the person who wants a million dollars will never get it. The person who has a vision to be a millionaire-type person will have the millions. There's a big difference. I want to become a millionaire inside of me.

Thinking like a millionaire, acting like a millionaire will make a difference. Once you become a millionaire inside of you, the money will follow. All of a sudden, the physical manifestation begins to come into your life. Just having a vision of a millionaire will never make it happen. Have a vision of who you want to become. That will always make it happen.

Have a clear, concise vision of who you want to be. Remember, the clearer the vision, the faster you will get there.

In 21 days you will know exactly where you want to go, and in a matter of time you will reach your destination, your destination being your dreams and desires.

System of Success (S.O.S.)
Exercises:

Write out your ideal you. Be very specific about what you want to be. Include what you want to be in relationships, in finances and in your spiritual walk. At the end of your life, specifically who do you want to be, and what personal qualities do you want to be remembered for?

Ideal you:

CHAPTER 11:

Where Are You At?

"I've arrived at this outermost edge of my life by my own actions. Where I am is thoroughly unacceptable. Therefore, I must stop doing what I've been doing."
—Alice Koller,

We examined where you are going. Now let's find out where you are at.

If I want to drive to San Diego, it is impossible for me to get directions if I do not know where I am at now. If you go to MapQuest, the first thing it asks is, "Where do you want to go?" The second thing is, "Where are you?" Without knowing where you are, you have no idea how to get to the destination.

My mom and I flew to Houston to visit Joel Olsteen's church. My assistant had given us driving directions that supposedly covered all of our travels.

I pulled out the one that was labeled "From airport to hotel," and we began our journey. Forty-five minutes later, it seemed that we had left the city. We were driving in the country looking for a Hilton Hotel. I thought it was weird, but no big deal.

Finally we reached the destination—a big building in the middle of nowhere. I guess it kind of looked like a hotel. I walked in and I was pleasantly surprised to see pictures of Joel up at this hotel. Of course after walking around for twenty minutes, I found a janitor who got a big laugh out of the question, "Where do I check in?" and, "Can you help me with my luggage?" Yes, the map was from the airport to the church.

In the midst of all my maps, I had no map that was from the church to the hotel. I had lots of maps to the hotel, but none from the church. We set out again.

You must understand that the hotel is five minutes from the airport and we were now one hour and thirty minutes into our search. We drove for another hour and a half and we still hadn't found it.

Finally, Mom called the hotel to ask for directions. While battling the traffic on the evil freeway that circles Houston like a vulture, I heard Momma and the hotel man talking. I could tell the man asked my mom, "Where are you?"

My mom looked out the window and began to tell him what we were passing. "Okay, we just passed a gas station, and we just passed a Burger King. It looks like there is a big sign advertising a legal firm." Long pause. "What do you mean you can't tell me how to get there?"

I sarcastically said, "Mom, tell him we just passed a blue car. That might help."

Innocently she said, "No, nothing will help him. He is useless."

You can't get to your destination if you don't know where you are.

It is the same with your life. Before you can get where you are going, you have to know where you are at.

The second part of your self-concept is your self-image. Your self-image is where you are at. What type of person are you? In relationship to where you want to go, where are you? Are you a problem solver? Are you good about managing your time? Do you know the industry? Do you have self-control? Are you a risk taker?

> **Innocently she said, "No, nothing will help him. He is useless."**

At the end of this chapter, I want you to write out where you are in relationship to where you want to go.

I want to go to San Diego. I am in Phoenix. Now that I know where I am and where I am going, I can prepare and decide what direction to go to get there.

You say you want to be a good husband. Where are you in regard to being a good communicator? Where are you in being a good listener? Do you treat your wife right? Do you take her out on dates? Do you treat her like a queen?

When you answer those questions, you can say, "This is where I am, and now that I know where I am and where I want to go, I can work out what I need to do to get there.

"I need to get some books on communication. I need to get some books on listening. I need to make a date with her this week." All of a sudden, you know what direction you must go in your life to get there.

The same principle applies to your finances. Ask yourself some questions. Where are you with your problem solving? If you're not very good, then you know that you need to get better. How are you with your time? If you find that you waste a lot of time, then you need to get good with your time. If you discover that you have a lot of fear inside of you, then you need to step out and take some risks.

We all have some areas that we know are okay. You are good at some things, so you really don't have far to go! You might need to change your friends and you definitely need to be willing to invest, but now that you know where you are, you can take that information and get to where you want to be in your life. You now have your vision, and your subconscious is working for you, taking you where you want to go in your life.

In a perfect world this would work easily. The problem is that many of you are like my mom. You don't know where you are in the Houston of your life. I have met with many bad husbands who thought they were great husbands. They thought they were great listeners, yet they were horrible.

I want you to find some brutally honest people to help you with this. It might be your mother-in-law, or it could be your mom or dad. It could be a critical friend. You want someone kind of mean who will really tell you where you are. Don't get mad. Don't get upset. It is to help you. You can't get to San Diego if you think you are in Las Vegas, but you are actually in Phoenix. The closer to reality you get, the faster you can get where you want to go.

> *"He that is taught only by himself has a fool for a master"*
> —Ben Jonson

Don't take what they say personally. Who cares? That might be who you were, but we are only concerned now with who you are becoming. You have to look beyond the meanness and find out how you can use it to get to where you want to go. The only reason you should get upset is if you plan on staying like that!

In 21 days we will be on the road from where we truly are today to our dreams and desires!

System of Success (S.O.S.)
Exercises

Exercise 1:
Copy your ideal self over from the previous chapter. You might save time by photo copying it twice. Now give those two copies to the brutally honest people in your life and ask them to write down next to what you've written where they think you are in relationship to your ideal. Don't worry about the small first blank. We will come back to that.

	Where I am Going: Ideal Self	Where I am at: Self-Image

	Where I am Going: Ideal Self	Where I am at: Self-Image

Exercise 2:

Now I want you, with an open heart, to look over what they wrote about you. Don't be defensive and don't get mad. It is a tool to help you. Read it over and over until you can see why they formed this perception about you. Remember, you are responsible for you. What do you need to work on? It doesn't matter that you think you are a great listener if no one around you thinks so.

Now I want you to go back and fill in the self-image, using what you believe and what the others believe. Remember, the closer you can pinpoint where you are at, the faster you will get to where you want to go.

I now want you to number each item on a scale of 1-10. One means it's not too important to change. You are pretty close already. Ten means you better change it right away. It is keeping you from your ideal self.

Every three months, I want you to redo this exercise. You may tweak and change your ideal self. As I said, there may be some small detours along the way. But it is good that you see you are heading toward that goal.

	Where I am Going: Ideal Self	Where I am at: Self-Image

	Where I am Going: Ideal Self	Where I am at: Self-Image

	Where I am Going: Ideal Self	Where I am at: Self-Image

	Where I am Going: Ideal Self	Where I am at: Self-Image

CHAPTER 12:

Dad, How Much Further Till We Are There?

People spend a lifetime searching for happiness; looking for peace. They chase idle dreams, addictions, religions, even other people, hoping to fill the emptiness that plagues them. The irony is the only place they ever needed to search was within.

—Romona L. Anderson

The third part of your self-concept is your self-esteem. We have determined where you are and where you are going. Now self-esteem is the distance between the two.

Your self-esteem is how far you have to go before you become your ideal self. If it is a long way, it can really make you feel down about yourself. But that is only if you are not moving toward it. That is a key element you will see in this chapter. You have felt down on yourself for years because you were going nowhere. As soon as you found out where you wanted to go and where you were at, how did you feel? You felt good. You were headed in the right direction.

The closer you get to your ideal self, the better you will always feel about yourself. It is a gauge that is supposed to help you get there, but for many, it has been something that held them back.

Self-esteem, in a nutshell, is the value that you put on yourself. How valuable are you? Do you like yourself? Do you love yourself? How valuable do you see yourself?

> *"Love yourself first and everything else falls into line. You really have to love yourself to get anything done in this world."*
> —Lucille Ball

It is interesting that the more you like yourself, the better you do, and the better you do, the more that you like yourself. It is an evil ride because the worse you do, the worse you feel about yourself, but the worse you feel about yourself, the worse you do. Our goal in this chapter is to get that cycle to stop working against you, and instead, get it working for you.

We are going to find out how we can reverse this, so we can start to like ourselves. We then do better, which makes us like ourselves even more.

Self-esteem is a very powerful force in your life. I could sit down with everyone reading this book, determine how much you like yourself and, based on that, tell you where you are headed in life. I can tell where you will be in three years, five years, ten years. I can tell whether you will be successful. I can tell whether you are a happy person or an unhappy person. I can do all of this based simply upon how much you like yourself. Nearly every psychologist agrees, your self-esteem determines your future.

If you were to think about your life, you would discover that everything you do and every decision you make are intended to raise your self-esteem or to keep from losing any more self-esteem. And that's why you won't step out and take certain risks. If you take a risk, you might fail. If you fail, you will lose your self-esteem. You can't step out and start a business because of your fear of losing self-esteem through failure.

> **The more you like yourself, the better you do, and the better you do, the more that you like yourself.**

If you really thought about it, really examined it, who cares if you fail? So you start a business and it goes under. Is it the end of the world? At least you tried. You learned and you try again. And you try again. And you try again. Until finally you find yourself in a multimillion dollar business.

> *"Success is the ability to go from one failure to another with no loss of enthusiasm."*
> —Sir Winston Churchill

What makes the great great? They keep trying. Michael Jordan missed more shots than he made. What if he said, "The odds are against me. What if I look like a fool? What if I miss again?" Do your best. Take the shot.

Imagine doing something where you failed seventy percent of the time. Most of us would never do that. Yet a good baseball player gets a hit only thirty percent of the time. Every strikeout is a lesson, something learned, something gained. Every at bat is another opportunity.

> *"Many of life's failures are people who did not realize how close they were to success when they gave up."*
> —Thomas A. Edison

In school growing up, I had a fear of failure. I thought that if I tried to get good grades but didn't, I would be a failure. But if I didn't try, well then, I'm not a failure, because I didn't try. So I got Cs and Ds in school.

As an adult, in my finances, I can be average all day. But when I try to become wealthy, what if I fail? That would make me a failure. And if I fail, I lose my self-esteem. Many of you suffer from the same thinking. You just want to be average. You only want to get by. You can do that and never fail.

If I try to make my marriage great and I don't, then I'm a failure, so I'm content with being just okay. I'm content with average finances and being an okay husband, because I have to protect my self-esteem. I have to protect it because I cannot lose anymore.

Your self-esteem is the distance between your ideal self and your self-image. This is why most people do not have a high self-esteem. They do not even know where their ideal self is. So the distance is so great that they don't even know how far they have to go.

For many years, people had been telling me to go to Rocky Point. They insisted that the ocean is amazing. The beaches are awesome. There is great golf, great fun.

To me, however, that is in Mexico, a long way. Why go there when I can go to San Diego, which is only a six-hour drive? Driving all the way to Rocky Point made no sense.

> Your self-esteem is the distance between your ideal self and your self-image.

Finally one year, my wife talked me into it. I got a map and figured it out. I discovered that it is only a three-hour drive.

For many people, wealth seems so far away. Happiness is so far away. Peace is too long of a drive. They continue to just settle for life. Their self-esteem stays the same because they are never headed toward what they want in life. If you just look at the map, however, you will discover that you are very close to wealth. Happiness is right around the corner. The closer you get, the better you feel about yourself. The better you feel about yourself, the faster you get there.

That's why, when you finished the last chapter, you were energized. You were excited. The juices were flowing inside of you. You had ideas pouring out of you. It's because you took a step toward your ideal self. Any time you read a self-help book or listen to a CD, when you take your wife out on a romantic date or you spend time with your kids, you feel better about yourself, because deep down, you know you are taking a step toward your ideal self!

That gauge is letting you know you are heading in the right direction. You now start to recognize when you make a wrong turn. Now that you know where you should go, that gauge will give you a warning when you get off the path. It has been a few weeks since you had a date night with your wife; something in you says, "Come on." You don't feel good about yourself in that area. So you call your wife. "Hey, I made some reservations at..." Now you feel good.

It works with your vision. You are saving for an investment. You go out and buy a $300 purse you don't need. On the way home, there is a knot in your stomach. You don't feel good about yourself. You turn around, return the purse and you feel good again.

Many people just ignore the signs. They just push through the warnings.

In high school, my brother and his friends were coming home from a ski trip, driving Dave's jeep. Half way home, they noticed the temperature gauge on the jeep go past the red. They all assumed it just broke—until the engine blew up.

The point is, what good is a gauge if, when it tells you what you don't want to hear, you assume it is broken? Learn to listen to the gauge. It will tell you when you are off track. It reminds you, "Hey, we should listen to finance CDs on the way to work. What's up with this radio garbage?" Don't just push through it and ignore it. It is a warning, telling you that you are not heading in the right direction. Instead, listen to the CD. When you get out of the car, you will feel BETTER about yourself! You have increased your self-esteem.

My gauge is a bully. It says, "Hey! Get off that couch and talk to your wife. Hey, I don't care if she is wrong. Go make up. It is a stupid fight. Let her be right. So what if she says she told you something you know she didn't."

I have to respond and do something. "Sorry, Honey, I made a mistake. You're right." In the grand scheme of things,

> **They all assumed it just broke— until the engine blew up.**

what does it matter? I have come to the conclusion that in my marriage, I can either be right or I can feel right. I let Holly win the fight. Later that night, while lying in bed, I feel so RIGHT. I think to myself, "If this is what wrong feels like, I don't want to be right."

The ideal self will push me every time. "Hey, what are you doing on the couch again? You need to get up and get outside and play with your children." That vision pushes me to where I need to go in my life.

At the end of this chapter, I am going to have you do many of the things my mom did, things that got her to where she is today. They may seem kooky, but if it makes you a millionaire, who cares? They work! I ask you to just do them for 21 days. In 21 days, you will be a different person. These exercises are designed to help put the last eight chapters together in you. They might sound a little weird, but these are the things that my mom did to overcome some of the ways in which she was programmed. These are the things that I did to catapult me to where I am today.

In 21 days you will feel great about who you are, which in turn makes you do better in all you do, which makes you feel better about who you are, which then makes you do even better at all you do. In 21 days you will be cycling toward your dreams and desires!

System of Success (S.O.S.)
Exercises

Exercise 1:

For the next 21 days, I want you to speak this as many times as you can throughout the day. I want you to say, "I love myself!" Say it right now. "I love myself. I love myself. I love myself." I can't say that without smiling. Say it over and over and over again, especially when you want to feel down about yourself or life. Just remind yourself: "I LOVE MYSELF." If you say it enough, your subconscious will believe you. When your subconscious believes that you really do love yourself, it will change how you treat yourself.

A friend of mine showed up to go golfing with another friend and me. On his shoulder he was dragging what I would call the oldest, nastiest bag of clubs I have ever seen. I thought he picked them up at a garage sale on the way over. These clubs were old during the First World War. He walked over to me and tossed them on the ground. They crashed on the concrete, but who cares? They have little value, right?

We got to the first green and he pulled out this beat up putter. My other friend, who is a huge golfer, looked at it and said, "Is that a Ping putter?"

The first friend said, "Yep."

The second friend said, "Let me see that." He looked at it and said, "This putter says 'Scottsdale' on it. It is very rare. Worth probably $1,000."

You should have seen how my friend treated that putter then. He asked to borrow one of my club covers. How valuable he saw that club dictated how he treated it.

My question is this. Did the club increase in value from the time he showed up and when he discovered its value? No, it was always valuable. It's the same with you. You are priceless, but until you see yourself valuable, you will not treat yourself like you are valuable.

Exercise 2:

For 21 days, confess your ideal person when you get up and when you go to bed.

For 21 days, I want you to say what you want to be and what you want to do. Do it in first person. Get up in the morning and say, "I am smart. I am a risk taker. I am a problem solver. I am a great communicator. I listen to my spouse. I am happy. I am..."

This is what my mom did. She said every day, over and over, "I am an overcomer. I am smart. I can do all things. I have favor. I have peace. I have joy."

"But, Scot, this is not who I am."

We do not confess who we are. We confess who we will become.

Exercise 3:

Every day, go to a quiet place, and I want you to picture your ideal self. See it vividly in your mind. See yourself stepping out and taking that risk. See yourself solving problems. See yourself around people, and see them liking you. See yourself being patient. Whatever your ideal self is, picture yourself in that way. Develop that inside of you. If you deal with anger, picture how you will respond when you get annoyed.

> *"There's a law in psychology, if you form a picture in your mind of what you would like to be and you keep it and hold it long enough, you will soon become whatever it is that you see."*
> —William James

When you play it out over and over in your mind, your subconscious doesn't know that it didn't actually take place. You get a month of experiences with risk taking in a few moments in the morning. For the last

21 days, you have been this amazing risk taker. The subconscious says, "I guess we are a risk taker. Change what we do accordingly."

It sees you in your mind being who you want to be, and it says, "That's who we are." It's embedding that image on your self-concept.

Exercise 4:

Record a three-minute tape or CD of your voice confessing who you are becoming. Play it in your bedroom twenty-four hours a day, even when you are not there. If your spouse does not like it, use headphones. My mom will tell you this was one of the most important things she did to change what was going on inside of her. There is something powerful about hearing your own voice over and over again telling you who you are. "I am smart, I am confident, I am a problem solver, I can do anything I put my mind to..." It sounds kooky, but if it makes you a millionaire, why not try it for 21 days?

Exercise 5:

This is probably the most important exercise. Remove negativity from your life. I think that most people today deal with being negative because they allow negativity in. They surround themselves with negativity.

You can't expect to be surrounded by negativity and have positive come out of your life. What comes in is going to come out.

I personally cannot be around a negative person for more than ten minutes. We go out with a new couple every once in a while, and one out of three times, I find this negative person sitting next to me, droning on about how this is bad and that is bad, and the world is falling apart. Nothing is good. I get to the point where I just want to jerk the steering wheel of the Hummer and put it into a tree. Let's end this suffering right now.

I won't go out with them again. I will not. I can't be in that world. That world makes me mad. That world makes me angry. I cannot be in a negative world.

Even if you are not a negative person, most of you reading this book start your day and end your day with negativity. You start and finish your day finding out about all the failures of society, the country, the world. You find out about everything bad that happened yesterday, everything bad that is going to happen today, tomorrow, and the rest of the year.

Most people get up in the morning and turn on that constant negative news called CNN. What a great way to start off your day. Let's find out about all the failures, all the wrong things, all the bad things that have happened all over the world. Let's get all that negativity inside of us. Let's feed our minds with that and wonder why we are negative throughout the day. Let's go to bed at night watching the news, get all that negativity inside of us and go to sleep, and for the next eight hours, allow our subconscious mind to feed on that information. Then we will wonder why we get up in the morning down and depressed.

It's not going to take you to your self ideal. You tell me which person is headed toward their ideal self. Is it the one who feeds on the negative news, or the one who gets up, puts in a self-help CD, and sits down and reads a good book on finance? Who put encouragement in his/her heart? Who put in despair? Who allowed fear in? Who put in confidence? Who allowed stress in?

In the morning, what you focus on is the rudder for your ship of the day. Where you end up most of the time is dictated by those first moments of the morning.

Which one is better? The one that is taking you to your ideal self or is it the one that feeds your fears, that feeds your worries, your stresses, and your anxieties? Choose the negativity and it holds you back, preventing you from taking any risks. You wonder why you can't step out? It's because for an hour a day, you listen to all the reasons why you shouldn't step out, all the reasons why things aren't going to work.

We wonder why we are so negative and down, why over fifty percent of Americans have to take some sort of drug to help cope with depression. I watch one news episode, and I am ready for some emotionally numbing drugs myself.

I don't watch the news. For the past five years, I have watched no news. Guess what? I have an amazing life. Not once have I said, "I wish I knew about all the murders yesterday." Anna Nicole died and that is very sad, but I didn't find out until a week later. Yes, it was sad, but knowing about it the day it happened wouldn't have changed anything.

Not watching the news didn't keep me from wealth. It helped me get to it. It didn't negatively affect my marriage. My marriage is better from it. I'm a better dad, a better person, with a better life. My life is amazing. I don't need to know information that is not pertinent in my life because anything that is going to hinder me from my success, I will remove.

I want the same for you. To be successful in life, you have to be positive. To be positive, you cannot allow in the negative.

Try it for 21 days. For 21 days, don't watch any news or read any newspapers. If you can skip to the up beat sections of the paper, that is fine—movies, community, life—just stay away from the negative.

That time you used to spend on the news, spend moving toward your ideal self. Read books, listen to CDs. In 21 days you will be surprised by how much further you are ahead than you would have been with that constant negative news holding you back.

CHAPTER 13:

What You Expect Out of Life, You Always Get

If you paint in your mind a picture of bright and happy expectations, you put yourself into a condition conducive to your goal.
—Norman Vincent Peale

Law #7: The Law of Expectation

The Law of Expectation:
What you expect with confidence becomes reality.

If you are a Christian, or an adherent to most other religions, then this law is known as the Law of Faith. What you expect with confidence, what you believe deep down inside, almost always comes into existence into your life.

What you expect out of life, you almost always get. What you expect out of your day, you get every single day. What you expect out of those around you, you always get. What you expect out of your children, you will get out of your children. If you expect them to obey you with a happy heart the first time you ask, they do. (This does not apply to want. Just because you want this from your kids, it does not change what you get.) If you expect your children to have to be told five times before they stomp off, slam the door and do what they were told, that is what you will get nearly every time.

There are women whose man runs around, is never home, doesn't have a job, and the woman just complains about it. She has that because of her expectations. My wife expects me to earn the income, expects me not to run around, expects me to be home most nights (occasionally I play racquetball or cards with the boys). She gets what she expects. If I went out to the bar one night, I would expect I will be all by myself. What she expects is what she gets.

My wife will counsel women who are attached to bums, and that is what she tells them. Don't put up with it. Raise your expectations. If he wants to be blessed with you, these are the new expectations of the marriage. He will either man up or get out. If he gets out, replacing a bum isn't all that hard to do. You haven't lost much.

"But, Scot, what happened to being responsible for yourself?" That is exactly what you did. You changed inside of you the perception of what you are worth in the relationship. You changed in you what you expected in the marriage. This is, of course, for big things. If he leaves the toilet seat up, pees on the floor and leaves his socks around, but is a great husband otherwise, focus on the good.

"As your consciousness expands, your level of expectation will grow. Keep asking yourself, am I selling myself short? Most of us are."
—John R. Spannuth

What you expect out of your income is what you will get. Once again, it's not what you want, but what you expect. Right now, what you are currently making is what you expect. If you are making $45,000 a year and you lost your job, you would go out and find another job that would be right around $45,000 a year. If not, it won't be long before that is what you are making.

What you expect with confidence will always happen in your life.

You could quit everything you are doing and move up to Alaska and within just a few months, you would get back to making $45,000 a year (plus that huge oil tax break of $6,000). What you expect with confidence will always happen in your life.

> *"Whatever we expect with confidence becomes our own self-fulfilling prophecy."*
> —Brian Tracy

Let me show you how this works. Your expectations motivate you from the inside out and drive you to what you expect. I ask my kids to do something and they do it, with a happy heart. (Understand I am not Hitler. My home is full of love.) But I will say, "Laken, when you get done with that show, please clean up the kitchen."

Ninety-nine out of one hundred times, he says, "Sure, Dad." One out of one hundred times, he says, "It's Heath's turn."

"I still need you to do it, Son."

"Okay, Dad." he replies.

If he ever says, "NO!," or throws a fit (this happens at two years old), that motivates me to bring change into his life. This involves using good parenting skills, of course, none of which I will share here. You have to buy my parenting program for that (www.trainupaparent.com).

Most parents ask the three-year-old, the three-year-old throws a fit, and the parents either threaten five times until finally the kid stomps off and does it, or the parents bribe or bargain with the kid. They told the kid five times to clean up. Finally the mom goes over and cleans up for the kid. I have never had to do that. Why? Because of what I expect.

You are driven and motivated by what you expect. If you expect tomorrow to be a bad day, then what happens in your life? You get up in the morning and you have to hit the alarm five times because your body is so tired. You drag out of bed and stub your toe. There's no stupid towel in the bathroom. You can't find the toothpaste. The kids used up all the hot water. You come downstairs. Your spouse picks a fight with you (probably because you came downstairs in another bad mood, but of course it is not your fault). You fight traffic to get to work. Your attitude and mood has stifled any creativity you could possibly have. You can't think clearly. You can't solve problems or be productive. You get into work and your boss treats you like a nothing. The boss has you doing things that are not in your job description. You watch the clock, hoping the day will end. You drive home again, stressed out about traffic and what waits for you at home. Home is so down and depressing, you want to just get away into TV land. You finally get into bed, and it was once again a bad day.

You got exactly what you expected!

> *"What we see depends mainly on what we look for."*
>
> —John Lubbock

Every day, I expect my day to be great! If you do like Scot Anderson does, your day will be great, too. When I get up in the morning, I don't need any coffee or anything else. I am excited about my day. I am excited about all the amazing opportunities that are in front of me. I may have problems, may run out of hot water, not find a towel, but cir-

I have never had to do that. Why? Because of what I expect.

cumstances do not dictate my day. I do. I come downstairs with a smile on my face, kiss the queen of my castle, talk to my kids about the awesome day before us, and send them off to school, ready to conquer the elementary world they are in. Traffic is no big deal, because I am listening to my Robert Kiyosaki CDs. Take all day, traffic. It doesn't bother me. I am growing and becoming better by the minute. My mind becomes a creative force. I think with clarity. I'm able to solve problems, overcome obstacles. When I had a boss, any opportunity to help out the boss was just that—an opportunity. My job is to make him/her successful.

Whatever I can do to help with that, I am glad to do. I am confident in my day. I get home to my amazing family and spend time strengthening our relationships. I then go to bed. Once again, it was a great day.

What was the difference in our days? Just what we expected!

> *"Our circumstances answer to our expecta-*
> *tions and the demand of our natures."*
> —Henry David Thoreau

What you expect, you will always get. We think that what happens to us forms our expectations. No, your expectation forms what happens. You may want to write that down because that is good!

We think what we do forms our expectations. "Tomorrow will be a bad day." What do you mean? You haven't even started yet. How do you know it is bad? You might win the lottery, be randomly picked to star in a movie, get offered a dream job. You are expecting bad out of your day with no evidence of what is to come.

What you expect forms what happens. What makes this law so powerful is you have the power to change your expectations. If I change my expectations, I change what I get.

According to Law #1, you are responsible for your expectations. If you build it, they will come. If you will expect it, you will get it.

System of Success (S.O.S.)
Exercises

First, write a problem area of your life. It could be in marriage, with kids, with finances, relationships, with yourself, your day, your job, your happiness...

Really think about what your current expectations are in this area. Maybe you don't expect your husband to take you out. You may not expect your kids to listen to you. You expect your day to be bad. Write these expectations down.

Now write down your new expectations and what action you will take to make it happen. If it is an expectation that your kids listen the first time you speak, the action should be to get Scot's "Train up a Parent" program or another really good parenting program.

If you expect to make more money, what are you going to do to make that happen? Expectation without works is dead. Expectation without action is just a want. You want to make more money. Nothing is in you driving you. When you really expect it, there is always action behind it.

You can't just want a great day. No, you must expect it by putting action behind it. My action is that I wake up happy, excited, and energized. I force a smile on my face. I come downstairs happy. I am happy all day, even if I have to fake it. If you fake it long enough, you actually become it.

For the next the next 21 days, read over your new expectations. Get them down deep inside of you. Now sit back and watch as your activated faith creates your world.

Number 1:
Problem Area:

Current Expectation:

New Expectation:

Action plan:

Number 2:
Problem Area:

Current Expectation:

New Expectation:

Action plan:

Number 3:
Problem Area:

Current Expectation:

New Expectation:

Action plan:

Number 4:
Problem Area:

Current Expectation:

New Expectation:

Action plan:

Number 5:
Problem Area:

Current Expectation:

New Expectation:

Action plan:

Number 6:
Problem Area:

Current Expectation:

New Expectation:

Action plan:

For the next 21 days, go over your new expectations.

CHAPTER 14:

No Such Thing as Bad Attitude, Only Bad Expectations

"Everything can be taken from a man but one thing: the last of the human freedoms—to choose one's attitude in any given set of circumstances, to choose one's own way."
—Viktor Frankel

Law #8: The Law of Attitude

The Law of Attitude:
> *You have complete control over your attitude*
> *by controlling your expectations.*

In the previous chapter, you learned you have control over your expectations. Since I have control over my expectations and my expectations control my attitude, this means I also have control over my attitude. My attitude determines how I respond, react, and choose in circumstances. This of course determines the life I live. Which means I control my world, by controlling my expectations, which controls my attitude.

If I expect tomorrow to be a bad day, I wake up tomorrow with a bad attitude. My expectations determine my attitude. I then go throughout the day, producing a bad day with my bad attitude. I go to bed yet again having lived the bad day I expected.

"The greatest discovery of any generation is that a human being can alter his life by altering his attitude."
—William James

Let's just go to a level where we live. Men, let's say your wife says, "Hey, we are going to a wedding tonight," and you respond with, "Oh I don't want to go to a wedding tonight. I want to go out to a movie or something fun; I don't want to get around all those boring people and dress up." You expect a boring, stupid night and you show up with a bad attitude.

Your expectation determined your attitude. But you can switch your expectation and say, "You know what, I can meet and talk to some new people, spend some time with my wife. It is important to her, so it is important to me. It is going to be romantic. Maybe we will even go out afterwards." All of a sudden, you changed your expectation, which changed your attitude.

In the first example, you show up with a bad attitude. You see everything through bad attitude goggles. By the end of the night, it was a horrible experience. You got what you expected. In the second example, you show up with a good attitude. Your wife and you are joking around, holding hands, being romantic. You meet some new people. By the end of the night, you had a good time. You got exactly what you expected.

What happened? You changed what you had the power to change—your expectation—which changed your attitude. You can't change the wedding; you can only change one thing—you.

Ladies, let's say you're driving home after running a million errands because your lazy husband is once again on the couch. You know that when you get home, the house

> **All of a sudden, you changed your expectation, which changed your attitude.**

will be a wreck, the kids a mess, nothing done all day. Your husband, of course, will call you a nag, among other things, and say how hard he works. How hard you work isn't even a consideration. You dread going home.

Or you are driving home after doing some important things for the family. You had a chance to get out of the house, listen to some CDs, unwind a little, while your husband has the kids. When you get home you will spend some much needed family time, turn off the TV, play some games, maybe get some ice cream, of course, after you do some house cleaning as a family. Your husband probably will be on the couch, but you know how to coax him into helping out. Men are such simple creatures. A kiss and a whisper of what's to come, and you know you could get him to re-shingle the house today. You go home excited about the day.

In example one, you get home to exactly what you expect. You can't take it anymore, and you let everyone have it. Your husband gets off the couch to pick up and help, but he mutters under his breath what you are. The kids are mad, your husband's mad, and you're mad. But you have a right to be mad. Nobody appreciates all that you do. Maybe they would if you were gone. After fighting all day with your husband, you climb into bed, dreading tomorrow. You got exactly what you expected.

In example two, you get home with a smile on your face and a kiss for all who are there. The house does need some help, so you go over and kiss the couch potato, whisper things that would make your father pass out, and ask him to help. He jumps up and off he goes. You let the kids know the plan. They will help clean, and then family game time with ice cream later. That night, after a day building relationships with your family, you climb into bed looking forward to another great day. You got exactly what you expected.

You changed what you had the power to change. You can't change the fact that lazy couch potato boy is lying around. You can change your attitude, which changes how you respond, which changes the outcome.

Get this. It is very important! Expectations have no evidence whatsoever. Read that again. Expectations are not based on evidence of the future. They are based on your assumptions of the future. You don't know for sure if it is going to be a bad day. You don't know for sure that when you get home it will be an awful experience. Tomorrow you might win the lottery. You might get home and your husband cleaned the whole house (the odds are better on the lottery). There is no evidence for your expectation. You make up in your mind what you think is going to happen. I just showed you how you could change the outcome by simply changing your attitude. If I change what I think is going to happen, I get different things to happen.

Expectations produce your attitude, which then produces your result. You expect average, though you have no evidence that today is just an average day and that you are just going to get by. But because you expect it, you have an average day. You expect a bad day. You have no evidence that tomorrow is going to be bad, but because you expect it, it becomes bad.

> **Expectations are not based on evidence of the future. They are based on your assumptions of the future.**

What if you were to change your expectations for tomorrow? You expect a great day. It changes your attitude, changes how you think, respond, and react throughout the day. At the end of the day you had a great day!

What you expect with confidence, you will always get! I challenge you. In 21 days, we are going to change our expectations. Every morning is a great day! Now you get up in the morning and you're energized! You go to the office and you're excited. Your mind is open. You're doing a lot better work, a lot better things. People are treating you differently because you're treating them differently. You get home at night and you expect a great night with your spouse.

Men, you are driving home thinking about the nag that will be waiting there for you. She will be mad because you want to watch TV and relax. After all, you reason that you earned it. Sure enough, after another fight, you go to bed for another bad night.

Instead, change your expectation. "Tonight will be awesome. I get to go home to the greatest thing to ever happen to me. There are millions of people who wish they had someone to go home to. I get to. I get to talk to her, find out about her day. I get to spend some time with my amazing kids. I better spend the time now, because before long, they are out of the house." You get home, smile on your face and hugs in your arms. You bring a different atmosphere into the home than you used to. Your wife is smiling, and before long you are talking like you used to when you were dating. After twenty minutes, she says, "Let me finish dinner. Why don't you go and relax a little bit?" That's something she used to fight you on. That night, as you climb into bed, you think about what an amazing night it was. What did you change? Your attitude!

When you come home and you have a bad attitude, who wants to be around you? And you wonder why you have a bad marriage. Change your expectations and it changes your attitude, changes what you do, and it changes what motivates you. All of a sudden, you change what is happening in that area of your life.

It works all of the time. I expect a great day. I always have one. You can look at any of my days and say. "But this happened to you." It doesn't matter what happened. It was a great day! Every day I expect to be a great day is a great day. It doesn't mean I don't have problems and situations. People who expect a bad day focus on the four or five bad things that happen and block out the one hundred amazing things that also happened. Your subconscious mind will always block out the things that don't go with what you expect.

The truth is that I can't even remember the bad things that happened last week. There may have been fifty bad things that happened, but I can't tell you what they were. However, I can tell you all of the amazing awesome things that happened. There are a lot more great things that happen during the course of every day, but because you expect a bad day, your mind will not allow you to see them. When you change your expectation, at the end of the day, you're able to say, "Look at all the awesome things that happened."

> You bring a different atmosphere into the home than you used to.

The Expectation Twist

I have learned that wealthy people, successful people, have the ability to twist their expectations so that they can keep a positive attitude even in bad outcomes. I believe that it is one of the most important things you can learn to do.

> *"We who lived in concentration camps can remember the men who walked through the huts comforting others, giving away their last piece of bread. They may have been few in number, but they offer sufficient proof that everything*

can be taken from a man but one thing: the last of the human freedoms—to choose one's attitude in any given set of circumstances, to choose one's own way."

—Viktor Frankl

Notice that in my previous examples about work, the wedding, the lazy husband and nagging wife, we didn't change the circumstances. We twisted our expectations. The lazy husband will be on the couch. You can't change that. You have to go to the wedding. You can't change that. Your wife will want some quality time. You can't change that. You can only change your expectation. You change so that you expect your wife is going to let you watch TV. You expect your husband to be off the couch. Expecting to not go to the wedding probably won't happen, but you change so that you expect to enjoy it. Expecting no problems in your day won't happen, but you can expect to enjoy the day anyway and you can expect to easily overcome any challenges you face.

I don't want to confuse some of you. Your expectations don't change people. They change you and your attitude. This, in turn, changes the outcome for you in circumstances that have some unchangeable things in them. I will have problems tomorrow, but my attitude changes how they affect me and how effective I am at solving them. My wife will want to spend time with me. My attitude changes how we spend that time and how it affects me.

Look at circumstances in your life about which you have a negative attitude, and you twist your expectations to give you a positive attitude. For 21 days, that is what I want you to work on. Anytime you start feeling negative, sit back, look at your expectations and then twist them.

For most circumstances in my life, I subconsciously twist them. It has become a habit. I can get a whole mess of problems in one day, yet still believe it is a great day. I twist it.

> Expecting no problems in your day won't happen, but you can expect to enjoy the day anyway.

Let me give you what is one of the most important twists you can do. Many people take no risks because they are afraid of failure. We all shy from certain things because of this fear of failure. But as you will see in later chapters, without risk, there is no reward. You cannot become a millionaire if you do not take huge risks.

But our attitude toward risks keeps us from taking them. We have an expectation that we will fail. What if we use the twist so that we never fail? Yes, I said it. You can live a life with no failure. I understand I am going against thousands of books with that statement. But it is true.

What is failure? Failure is when you do not get your desired outcome. You do something and you do not get what you expected. Remember, we have the power to change what? Expectation. Let's change our overall expectation for whatever we try. Let's change it to something we always get so we will never fail.

What do you always get when you try something? You always get a result. Every time you have ever tried something, you got a result. So if your new expectation is result, good or bad, you will never fail.

I have had a number of businesses go under. Did I fail? No! I got a result. I learned a great deal. I can take that $5,000 lesson into my next business. You can't buy that kind of education for $5,000. Do you see how, rather than take away from my self-esteem, it added to it? I learned. I grew. I got closer to my ideal self.

In life there are no such things as failures for you anymore, just outcomes. That divorce wasn't a failure. It was an outcome. Hopefully you learned what YOU could have done differently, and you will take that into your next relationship. You got fired. That wasn't a failure. It was an outcome. Hopefully, you learned what YOU could have done differently, and you take that into your next job. That business that went under was not a failure, it was an outcome.

You just took something negative in your life and you twisted the expectation part of it. You can take problems and call them opportunities. That changes your attitude toward them. A fight with your spouse is an opportunity for you to learn. Okay, what could you have done differently? Someone says something not so nice. It could be a spouse or a close friend. Don't allow it to affect you. You know who you are and who you are becoming. You look at it from a positive expectation. Is there truth in it? Do you need to change? Well then, it was a very helpful comment. Incorporate the change in your life and say, "Thank you very much." Maybe it is them. They are going through some things. This allows you to be a better friend. Once again, "Thank you very much."

> *"Everything can be taken from a man but...*
> *the last of the human freedoms—to choose one's*
> *attitude in any given set of circumstances, to*
> *choose one's own way."*
>
> —Victor Frankl

Reasonable Expectations

One of the things you must remember about expectations, and follow me on this, is that we have to have what I call reasonable expectations. The only time we get mad in life is when our expectations are not met. Remember our goal for expectations is not to get upset.

But the only time we get mad is when our expectations are not met. Let me give you and example. Every day on the way to work, you expect traffic. You don't like it, but what can you do? It is a Saturday and you want to go to the mall. You expect no traffic. Wouldn't you know it, bumper to bumper. You are so mad. It's the same circumstance as every other day, just different expectations.

> In life there are no such things as failures for you anymore, just outcomes.

Your wife calls you and says, "Honey, I went down to Victoria's Secret and, when you get home tonight, I'm going to rock your world. You may want to pick up a power generator on the way home. Tonight is going to be like no other.

I guarantee we will break laws in seventeen states." I am so excited I can't even drive. My expectations have given me an amazing attitude. I run in the door, and I am nude before I get to the steps. I rush into the bedroom and she is sleeping, fully dressed in a jogging suit. I might go to prison on that night. Unfulfilled expectations can make you crazy.

When we set up our expectations, we need to have reasonable expectations. Once again, it is not reasonable for you to think everything you do will make money, or that any business you start will become an instant million-dollar business. That is unreasonable. It's not reasonable for you to think everything in life will always turn out perfect. If you think that, you will live a very frustrated life.

You have to have reasonable expectations in life. I expect to win at whatever I do. To me, winning is playing my best, and if my score isn't the highest, sure, in a sense I lost. But I twist it so that I feel like I won if I learned from the game. Now I know what to work on and how to become better. But for a person to think he will always win, this is the person who smashes his tennis racquet into a million pieces after a loss. He had an unreasonable expectation.

> *"Winning isn't everything, but wanting to win is."*
> —Vince Lombardi

I expect every business I do to be a success. And they all are because of the twist. Even though in a financial sense, some of them had to be shut down, they were still a success because I got an outcome. If you think every one of your businesses is going to make you rich, you are in for a very upsetting journey. That is unreasonable.

With the twist, however, every day is good. All that I do has a great outcome. This keeps building my self-esteem. It keeps me taking risks until finally I step into that billion-dollar company.

With unreasonable expectations, you ultimately give up, quit and you live a very miserable life.

System of Success (S.O.S.)
Exercises

I want you to list some areas in your life where you have had a bad attitude. Then let's put a twist on them to change your attitude. How can we change your expectation for that event so your attitude will change? Consciously, for 21 days, constantly remind yourself of your new expectations. In the morning, on the way to work, during the day, on the way home, remind yourself of your new expectations, over and over, until that thinking pattern becomes a habit.

If going to work is something you hate, how can we twist what you expect out of work so that you end up excited about it? "It's an opportunity to make money I can invest. If I work hard, I can get a raise and all of my raise goes to my future business. I have the opportunity to be the best at my job, do things no one else has ever done." Do this for all areas of life—marriage, failure, whatever it might be. Let's become positive people, happy people, excited-about-life people. You have the power to do so. Just give me 21 days. Also come back here whenever you find yourself with a bad attitude, and do this exercise for whatever that attitude is.

Area You Have Bad Attitude	Current Expectations	New Expectations

CHAPTER 15:

Expect Nothing But the Best From Yourself

"Winning is not a sometime thing; it's an all the time thing. You don't win once in a while; you don't do things right once in a while; you do them right all the time. Winning is a habit. Unfortunately, so is losing."
—Vince Lambardi

We have been talking about your expectations. I have been dealing with changing what you expect out of things that in a sense are out of your control. I now want to spend some time changing your expectations of something you do control, the only thing in this universe that you have control over—you.

What you expect out of life from others and from society should be a lot different than what you expect out of yourself. Remember, what you expect, you usually get. You have been expecting to just get by, just do average, sit back and let life pass you by and that is exactly what you got.

Successful people have much higher expectations for themselves than the other ninety-five percent of the people out there. That is why they are successful. They get what they expect.

"Any fact facing us is not as important as our attitude toward it, for that determines our success or failure. The way you think about a fact may defeat you before you ever do anything about it. You are overcome by the fact because you think you are."

—Norman Vincent Peale

In 21 days, I want you to have a habit of high expectations out of yourself. "But, Scot, what about all that unreasonable talk?" That is for things out of your control. I want you to get upset at yourself when you are not going toward your ideal self. I want that passion to rise up and drive you to excellence. Yes, when expectations aren't met, we get upset. Good. Push yourself to excellence.

In 21 days, I want you to be in a place where you know that you can be successful at anything you give your heart to. It is what you expect. Notice the wording. It doesn't mean you are great at everything, just the things you put your heart to.

I want that to be what you really believe deep down. It's not arrogant. I do not want you to be arrogant and think, "I am better than others." Rather, I want you to think, "But I can be as good as anyone out there. I'm not better than anybody out there, but I can be as good as anybody out there."

It needs to be written on your subconscious that you can do anything that is before you. It is so set inside of you that anything that says you can't goes against what you expect, and it makes you upset. Nothing can tell you that you can't! Something rises up inside of you, something that used to say, "You can't," and pulled you down, now forces you up and says, "I can. I can be good at that," whatever that is.

This is what is in me. I want the same in you. Any problem that comes my way, something inside of me says, "I can solve that." That is what I want you to have inside of you. "I can solve that."

> **"I can be as good as anyone out there."**

"Scot, that is unreasonable to say you can solve all problems." Sure, I put a twist on it, because if there is no solution, then there is no problem. But the old Scot used to just ignore problems, hoping they would go away, or wait for others to solve them. The new Scot can't. I expect to overcome any problem (we call them opportunities). What is amazing is that I expect to overcome all problems, and guess what? So far I do! You can also.

> *"If there is no solution, we don't have a problem!"*
> —Unknown

I believe in my heart that I can run any company in America. It's going to take a lot of work. I'm going to have to get a lot of knowledge if they give me IBM. I will have to put in a tremendous amount of time and effort. But I know if I put my heart to it, I can do it. Is that you? In 21 days, this will be you. And it will be this confidence (not arrogance) that will take your sales to another level, your company, your marriage, your life.

There is nothing I can't be and nothing I can't do if I put my mind to it. I believe it and I expect it. In seminars, I have people blurt out things to see if they can stump me on what I can do.

"Scot, how about playing on the PGA?"

If I wanted to be on the PGA, I know, if I gave my heart to it, I could be on the PGA. It would take me a couple of years. I would give eight hours a day to practicing. I would invest a lot of money in getting a great golf coach. In a couple of years, I really believe Scot Anderson could be on the PGA.

I had one smart aleck, say to the 5'4" Scot, "How about the NBA?"

This will blow your mind, but I believe I could. Muggsy Bogues was my height, yet thousands of 6'4" players were overlooked and he was chosen for the NBA. Why? He expected. He believed he could. My mind has even worked out the solution. You know what I would do? I would do the half court shots at the end of every quarter. I would spend eight hours every day shooting half court shots. Grab the ball, run to the half court line and shoot. It's amazing that your subconscious mind will do whatever you ask to the point of the limit you set on it.

A few years back they moved the three-point line closer. They thought that people would make more baskets. That did not happen. The players actually hit the same percentage of shots. You could move the three-point line all the way back to half court and I honestly believe that it would be the same percentage. Why? Because the mind will take you to whatever limit you put on it.

So here I am eight hours a day for two years practicing the half court shot. I believe that I could get good enough to make fifty percent of my shots. Understand that most NBA games are decided by four points or less. You bring Scot off the bench at the end of each quarter. I make half my shots and increase our score by six points a game. I have now taken my team to a different level and all I did was become great at one thing.

> **I would do the half court shots at the end of every quarter.**

My mind believes that whatever you put in front of it, I can do! That is where your mind needs to be in 21 days. Your expectations, with faith and confidence, will always produce it into your life.

> *"I don't say these things because I believe in the 'brute' nature of man or that men must be brutalized to be combative. I believe in God, and I believe in human decency. But I firmly believe that any man's finest hour—his greatest fulfillment to all he holds dear—is that moment when he has to work his heart out in a good cause and he's exhausted on the field of battle—victorious."*
>
> —Vince Lombardi

Expectation changes attitudes, which changes results!

One of my hobbies is strategy card games. I play a game called Marvel and DC VS. For those that read comics, you recognize Marvel and DC. This is a game where you take comic characters, put a deck together of sixty cards and then battle each other.

A few years back, some friends of mine started playing. I spent about eighty hours building my Fantastic Four deck. What a great deck this was. It never lost. In 200 matches, it may have lost five times. We went to a city tournament and I won that. We then decided to go to the big $10,000 national tournament with Scot's Fantastic Four deck.

It was a ten-game tournament to decide who moves into the top eight, second day tournament. The first four matches, I crushed my opponents. Then I found out that the best VS player in the world was there and he was doing deck analysis. I was so excited because there was no deck like this. I expected to show it to him, have him stand up yell "Stop trying to build the perfect deck, Scot has done it!!!"

I went over and handed him my deck and watched with eager anticipation as he went through it. Finally he looked up and said to me, "This deck is good, but it won't win VS Tier One decks." (Those are established winning decks.)

I said, "Yes it will."

He said, "No, it won't beat Teen Titan. It won't beat Sentinel."

I said, "But I beat two Sentinels today, and I beat a Teen Titan."

He said, "Let me explain the math to you."

Being a math guy, this interested me. He showed me that to beat those decks, I needed what is called a perfect draw. Then, yes, my deck is unbeatable. The problem is, he explained, mathematically, you will only get that draw maybe one out of ten times. The math was right on.

What I didn't realize was I expected a perfect draw and somehow I always got it.

I walked away discouraged and I had no confidence in this deck. The best I could hope

I expected to show it to him, have him stand up and yell, "Stop trying to build the perfect deck. Scot has done it!!!"

for was winning ten percent of the time. I lost every single match the rest of the day! I got the absolute worst draws I have ever seen. On one draw, I got no characters to battle at all. That's nearly impossible to get. That stupid deck has never won a match since. I hate my Fantastic Four deck.

I'm just making a point here. What was the difference? My expectations. I used to think I would always get a good draw, and I always did. I always won with that deck.

Just to brag, I put another deck together and took second in the nation on the next tournament. Why? Because I believe I can be amazing at anything I put my mind to. I could make $100,000 a year just playing this game if I wanted to.

Whatever I do, I can be successful at it.

System of Success (S.O.S.)
Exercises:

First, list limiting beliefs you have about yourself. Now list the new beliefs you are planning to have. For example:

I'm not book smart…I can be smart at anything I put my mind to.

Just like Daddy said, I don't have any common sense…I am very smart and I make great decisions all the time.

I'm not management material…Inside of me resides a great leader. I can manage. I can lead any team that is put before me. I have many great gifts and talents to help me lead. Anything I am lacking, I know I am a book or two away from possessing.

Go back to the Chapter 8 Exercises and do each of these exercises for this new belief.

Limiting Belief About Yourself:

Your New Belief:

Limiting Belief About Yourself:

Your New Belief:

Limiting Belief About Yourself:

Your New Belief:

Limiting Belief About Yourself:

Your New Belief:

Limiting Belief About Yourself:

Your New Belief:

Limiting Belief About Yourself:

Your New Belief:

Limiting Belief About Yourself:

Your New Belief:

Limiting Belief About Yourself:

Your New Belief:

Limiting Belief About Yourself:

Your New Belief:

Limiting Belief About Yourself:

Your New Belief:

Limiting Belief About Yourself:

Your New Belief:

CHAPTER 16:

You Are a Magnet

> *"You are a living magnet, drawing to yourself the people, the resources, and the ideas you need to fulfill what you expect. To the successful it is out of their faith, for others it is out of their fears. If you don't like what you attract, don't change what is coming towards you, change the magnet that is bringing those things into your life."*
> —Scot Thomas Anderson

Law #9: The Law of Attraction

The Law of Attraction:
> *You will attract the people, the ideas, and the resources that go with your most dominate thoughts and expectations.*

Basically, whatever you really believe, your subconscious will work at bringing you the tools you need to produce it. You are a living magnet. You attract the people, the ideas, and the resources you need to accomplish the expectations you have set within you.

Once again, your expectations are bringing your life to you, just like a magnet. Whatever is in your subconscious mind, the most dominant thoughts, the expectations that you have, your mind will attract.

Somehow my mind attracted the right cards in the VS game. Your mind will attract the people you need, the finances you need, the ideas you need, to fulfill your expectations.

If you expect a bad day, your mind will bring everything you need to fulfill that order. You expect a bad night with your spouse; serve it up hot, because here comes your order. If you change that, and expect a great day, you get what you ordered.

If you are full of fear about what the future holds, the future holds what you are afraid of. Fears are negative expectations. Your fears are attracting everything you need to produce that fear in your life. In the next chapter we will discuss how to get over those fears, but for now, I want you to be aware. They are producing. You need to get rid of every fear you have.

If you fear your business will go under, it will. But if you have a sense of confidence inside of you, you begin to attract the people and the ideas you need. It does not mean that your business is guaranteed to work, but it means that in the course of time, it seems like all of a sudden, you attracted the resources and the ideas you needed to catapult one of your businesses into success. It may be your first. It might be your seventh. But that confidence will bring success.

Your mind attracts what it needs to fulfill what is expected. What are you attracting into your life? What is the one thing you can change that will change what you attract? Your expectations!

CHAPTER 17:

No Pain No Gain!

*"I guess what I'm trying to say is, I don't think
you can measure life in terms of years. I think longevity
doesn't necessarily have anything to do with happiness.
I mean happiness comes from facing challenges and
going out on a limb and taking risks. If you're not
willing to take a risk for something you really care
about, you might as well be dead."*
—Diane Frolov and Andrew Schneider

Law #10: The Law of Risk and Rewards

The Law of Risks and Rewards:
> *There are no rewards in life without a risk.*
> *The greater the risk, the bigger the reward.*

There are no rewards without risks. I want you to say
that over and over again to yourself.

We are brought up in a society that teaches us to
wait for the rewards. There's no need for risks. So we
sit around waiting for Ed McMahon to show up with our
ten million dollars. We wait for the lotto numbers to
come through, the 401(k) to magically get to millions of

dollars. We wait for heaven to open up and God to drop money in our laps because the pastor said so.

IT DOES NOT WORK THAT WAY! It never has and it never will. The only way to get the reward is to take a risk! Say it again, and again, and again, until you really believe it.

> *"I don't want to find myself in a nursing home someday thinking that all I did was play it safe."*
>
> —Charlie Eitel,
> Chairman/CEO,
> The Simmons Company

This money for nothing attitude has kept us back. Subconsciously, you say, "Why step out? Money is going to come to us. We can get the rewards without a risk." And it never happens. You need your subconscious to say "HEY! We better take a risk or we ain't getting any reward!"

We have to have that trained inside of us. "I want rewards, so I better take a risk." No one plays Monopoly the way he lives his life because he would never win. Am I right or am I right? If you sat around taking no risks, you would get no reward and you would be out of the game very quickly.

I said it before. If you played life like you play Monopoly, you would be rich. You don't just sit around waiting for the "Pass Go." You buy, you risk, you put it all on the line. You don't let the last loss hold you back. "Well, I failed last time, so I am going to just play it safe, so I don't fail again." No, the last game doesn't affect this game. It's a new game, a new business. The only thing I bring from the past is what I learned!

> **No one plays Monopoly the way he lives his life because he would never win.**

Many of us play life to lose. For ten, fifteen, twenty years we're just going to play it safe. The market is not right. We don't know if it's going to work out. Would you ever win at Monopoly doing that?

How do you win? You've got to take risks! There are no rewards unless you take the risk. You're going to have to buy that property. You're going to have to step out and put it on the line. Oh it's going to be close and tight. It's going to be a risk. But you're going to put hotels on there. The reward is worth the risk.

> *"A minute's success pays the failure of years."*
>
> —Robert Browning

Have you ever played those tycoon games? I played Lemonade Tycoon the other day. I am amazed that just by selling lemonade, using the principles of this book, I could become a millionaire. You can make millions of dollars selling lemonade on this little game. I'll bet you that if you actually took it to real life and applied the same principles as you did on Lemonade Tycoon, and you went to New York and you started yourself a lemonade business, you would win in that area of your life. It would only cost you a few hundred dollars to get that business going.

IBM founder Thomas J. Watson was asked by a young up and coming man, "How do you succeed faster?"

I love this. He said, "You know what you have to do? You have to double the rate of your failure." That's deep. He said double the rate of your failure.

> *"If you want to succeed faster, you must double your rate of failure"*
> —Thomas J. Watson

In a sense, double the risks you are taking. Step out as much as you can. We live in that fear of failure. Here he is saying to attack it. Double it. The more you fail, the faster you become successful. The more you fail, the more likely you are to succeed.

The more things you try, which is going to be the Law of Probability, the more likely it is that you are going to succeed. If you want to succeed faster, you better double the rate of your failure. You better double the risks that you're taking. You are taking more risks, which gives you more chances to be rewarded in what you are doing.

I'll say it again. No risk, no reward. If I want reward, I have to take risks. The more rewards I want, the more risks I am going to have to take.

"A lot of people approach risk as if it's the enemy when it's really fortune's accomplice."
—Sting

System of Success (S.O.S.)
Exercises

On your recorder that plays twenty-four hours a day, with your voice, I want you to add the phrase, "There are no rewards without risks." I want you to hear this over and over. I want you throughout the day for 21 days to say this over and over. Every time fear steps in, you say, "There are no rewards without a risk." Get that down deep in your subconscious until your subconscious is screaming at you, "Hey, if we don't take this risk, we will get no reward!"

CHAPTER 18:

Fear—Your Greatest Enemy

> *"Cowards die many times before their deaths;*
> *The valiant never taste of death but once.*
> *Of all the wonders that I yet have heard,*
> *It seems to me most strange that men should fear;*
> *Seeing that death, a necessary end,*
> *Will come when it will come."*
> —William Shakespeare

What is keeping you from your dreams and desires? What is keeping you from doing what you know you should do? What force is your greatest enemy? Fear. Fear is the force in your life that is keeping you from taking the risks in your life that will produce what you desire.

> *"Our doubts are traitors,*
> *And make us lose the good we oft might win*
> *By fearing to attempt."*
> —William Shakespeare

Fear is a negative expectation. Expectations will always produce themselves. Either your faith is producing your desires, or your fears are keeping you from them. You have to understand that fear always produces itself.

You have a fear of failure, so you never step out and try anything. And at the end of your life, you lived far below your potential. That fear produced itself in your life.

"I have come to realize that all my trouble with living has come from fear and smallness within me."
—Angela L. Wozniak

If you want to be successful, getting rid of fear is one of the most important things you can do.

None of the other laws will matter if that fear holds you back from stepping out. No risk, no reward. Fear is the enemy of reward.

1. Admit.

"Admit that your own private Mount Everest exists. That is half the battle."
—Hugh Macleod,

The first step is to admit. Admitting it is half the battle. You cannot change what you don't know you have. You have to be honest with yourself. Sure, it hurts to say it, but when you admit it, you will feel a huge relief. Immediately you feel a weight lift off your shoulders. You know you are halfway there. Take responsibility. Remember you cannot change what you are not responsible for!

"The unexamined life is not worth living."

—Socrates

I had a fear of failure. So I thought that if I don't try, I am not a failure. If I don't try in school and I just get Cs, I am not a failure. So I never tried anything, and that made me a failure. I could not change it until I admitted I had it.

While you are trying to find out what fears you have, look at your life and areas that are not going the way they should. I guarantee there is a fear involved. If your marriage

---

Fear is the enemy of reward.

---

is not working out, what fear in you holds the marriage back? Or do you have a bad relationship with your kids? What is the fear in you?

"Aim for success, not perfection. Never give up your right to be wrong, because then you will lose the ability to learn new things and move forward with your life."

—Dr. David M. Burns

Also, I challenge you to go back to those two brutally honest people and ask them. They can point out some fears that you are too afraid to admit to. Once again, who cares what they are as long as we get rid of them?

Right now, I want you to write down the limiting fears in your life. It could be fear of failure, fear of intimacy, fear of death, fear of life, fear of people, fear of public speaking, fear of…Any fear you have that limits you, write it down. Admit you have the fear.

Write these down in the section at the end of the chapter.

2. Take control of your thoughts.

Go back to the Law of Substitution. You have to substitute faith for fear. You have to change that little recorder in your mind. I would say over and over, "I am a risk taker. I am a risk taker."

I would hear a voice, "What if you fail?"

I said, "There are no failures, just outcomes. I am a risk taker."

You do that for 21 days, and your mind starts telling you, "Hey, you are a risk taker."

I had a huge fear of heights. This was limiting my life. The kids would want to ride a rollercoaster. That's not for Dad. But I don't want to miss out on that. Plus I don't want any fear in my life. So I would tell myself over and over, "I'm not afraid of heights. I love heights. I love heights." I reprogrammed my subconscious mind.

You have to substitute for that fear in your mind. Remember, every thought is a seed. You cannot allow in one thought of fear.

Talk to yourself. "There's nothing to be afraid of. It's no big deal." Talk to yourself over and over again. "I'm not afraid to take risks." You say to yourself, "I can talk in front of people. I am great in front of people. I am funny in front of people." Once again, we confess what we are going to be and do and not what we are. "I am great at talking in front of people. I am confident. I am a risk taker. I am…" Whatever your fear is, you say in the first person that you are what you want to be. "I'm not afraid of heights. I love heights. I love to be up high. Put me up on top of a skyscraper and I will eat my breakfast up there every morning." I am confident that I am not afraid of heights.

> *"Since the great majority of people do not feel worthy and deserving of abundant good fortune, radiant good health and total success in all areas of their lives that overriding thought pattern controls the results people get. The first order of business of anyone who wants to enjoy success in all areas of his/her life is to take charge of the internal dialogue they have and only think, say and behavior in a manner consistent with the results they truly desire."*
>
> —Sidney Madwed

3. Picture yourself doing that which you are afraid of.

Remember, we talked about the power of being able to picture yourself. Every time you picture yourself doing something, your subconscious does not know it didn't actually happen. By the time I went to take my first helicopter ride, my subconscious thought we had already been on a hundred of them. "We do this thing every day. No big deal."

You close your eyes and you see yourself speaking in front of people. You are confident. You are funny. You see yourself signing those papers for that land. It feels good to step out.

When your mind sees you over and over again, then it says, "Oh, we can do this. There's no reason to be afraid!" It begins to remove that fear from inside of you.

> *"Formulate and stamp indelibly on your mind a mental picture of yourself as succeeding. Hold this picture tenaciously. Never permit it to fade. Your mind will seek to develop the picture...Do not build up obstacles in your imagination."*
> —Norman Vincent Peale

4. Write down the consequences.

What happens if I don't get rid of the fear? I think it is really good to write down what you miss out on. If I don't take a risk and start a business, I will be stuck working a dead end job. If I don't step out and take a risk in a relationship, I will end up lonely and by myself. Now, anytime that fear comes up, remind yourself.

Write down the consequences under each fear at the end of the chapter.

5. Consider the worst case scenario.

What is the worst that could happen by doing what you are afraid of? Considering a worst case scenario always helps me with my fears.

Say I am going to buy my first million dollar investment. I can feel that fear well up inside of me. What is the worst case scenario? I have to go bankrupt. I lose the land and some money. I still have my house, my awesome wife, my kids, my health. I will take what I learned and do it again. When you really break it down, it isn't that bad.

> "Formulate and stamp indelibly on your mind a mental picture of yourself as succeeding."

When I first started speaking in front of people, my mind would say, "What if you forget what you are going to say? What if you look like an idiot?"

I would say to myself, "The worst case scenario is I screw up and I forget what to say. Everybody in here is an adult. I probably will get a lot of compassion out of it. I will learn from it, and be better next time. Not that big of a deal." The fear left. It has no place here.

You have a fear of being hurt in a relationship. You step out, give your heart to someone, and, the worst case, they break it. You say, "It's no big deal. We had a bunch of good times in the interim. I take what I learned and try again. I know I am a great catch, an amazing person and someone out there will be lucky enough to enjoy me. But if I don't risk, I will die lonely."

> *"The greatest mistake you can make in life is to be continually fearing you will make one."*
> —Elbert Hubbard

6. Challenge the truth of the fear.

"If the truth will set you free, that means a lie will hold you in bondage."
>   —Scot Thomas Anderson

The truth will set you free, but a lie will hold you in bondage. There are so many fears inside of you that are based on things that are not true. You fear relationships because all men are jerks. Your dad was a jerk. You had many jerk boyfriends. But that is a false belief that you need to challenge to help you get over your fear. If you hold onto that lie, it will keep you from great things you can be experiencing in this life. That lie keeps you in bondage.

When I grew up and for whatever reason, my dad put in my heart that if you rode a subway, you would die. I saw some TV shows about gangs in the subway. I saw movies about it. People who ride subways get mugged and killed all the time. You laugh at that, but all of us have silly things inside of us that are not true.

Wealthy people say, "Why are you afraid of starting a business? Why do you have this fear? Why are you afraid to speak in front of people?" For me, the subway was my silly fear.

Holly and I went to Chicago and she wanted to ride the subway. I'm appalled. "Honey, I'm not dying today. I promise you that! No, we are not going on the subway!" A huge fight followed. She called me some non-manly names. I don't care. I'm not dying today.

One day, while going through my fears, this one came up. I began to think about it. Does it make sense that subways could be that bad and the police would not do anything about it? Would anyone get on it if it was true? I then got on the Internet and looked up statistics. I found out you are more likely to get car jacked than mugged on a subway.

> The truth will set you free, but a lie will hold you in bondage.

We went to Boston, and you should have seen my wife's face when I said, "Let's ride the subway." I really had to fight that fear on the way down there. But sure enough, we got on the subway. No gangs, no killings. Just a bunch of nice people enjoying the ride. For years, I had been missing out because of a stupid fear.

You have a stupid fear that is holding you back. It could be flying on an airplane, speaking in front of people (a much needed gift to really be successful in life), relationships…

There are things in your life that could add a great deal of greatness to you, but you've been afraid of them because you didn't have truth in you! Get the truth about it! Research it! You'll find out that what you feared wasn't true. You'll say, "Oh my gosh! I didn't know that. Okay, I have some wrong things inside of me!" The truth will set you free!!!

> *"Nothing in life is to be feared, it is only to be understood. Now is the time to understand more, so that we may fear less."*
> —Marie Curie

7. Know that in the end you win.

"If you know you win in the end, there isn't much to be afraid of!"
—Scot Thomas Anderson

That really helps me. When I know that in the end I am successful, I have no fear of what happens in the meantime.

Sure, I might stink at this first public speaking, but I will learn and grow and do it again—and again and again. And in the end I know I will be really good.

My first business may fail. My second might fail. My third, my fourth… But I know if I start enough businesses, I will step into a successful one. Who cares about the first five if the sixth makes me a millionaire?

"You always pass failure on the way to success."
—Mickey Rooney

When you know that in the end you win, all that happens in the middle doesn't matter! In January 2007, the Colts were playing New England in the playoffs. Being a huge Colts fan, I was excited. Of course, I happened to be out speaking on the day of the game. Thank God for His second greatest gift to mankind—TiVo. I recorded the Bears game and the Colts game.

I got home that night and watched the Bears game because I didn't want the Colts game to give me the Bears score. I decided I would watch the Colts game the next night. I got up in the morning, excited about the prospect of a night of Colts football. I had told all those around me not to let me know the score so I could enjoy it. I told everyone, that is, except for my children. Of course, at breakfast that morning, my six-year-old said, "Dad, can I have Capn' Crunch? Oh yeah, Dad, the Colts won."

> **If I start enough businesses, I will step into a successful one.**

After I grounded Baylor for a year, off to work I went. That night I still decided to watch the game.

If you remember the game, the Colts got down by eighteen points at half. Normally, I would be going nuts, screaming at the TV, "You idiot, Peyton Manning. What are you thinking? Can we not fumble the ball? You do make seven million dollars a year. That is not too much to ask."

But instead, I sat calmly on the couch watching. Why? I knew the end. It didn't matter what happened during the game if in the end we win. Go ahead, throw another interception. Fumble the ball. In the end we win. I have no stress, no worry.

It was the fourth quarter, we were still down fourteen points. No big deal. We had one minute left. We were still losing. No big deal, because in the end we win.

Something that normally would have been a huge stressful event, was just a peaceful night of football. Why? Because I knew in the end we win!

What if the coach of the Colts played the game like we play life? What if he said, "We are down by eighteen points. I can't take another failure. We are going to just play it safe. I hope to get out of here down only eighteen points."

No! No risk, no reward. We have to take bigger chances, bigger risks. Keep throwing that ball. Another interception? Okay, what did we learn? Let's do it again.

They won because they took risks. It's the same as in your life, when in the end, you know that you win. It does not matter what happens in the meantime. Keep reminding yourself, "In the end, I win."

Your mind says, "What if the business goes under?"

You say, "I will start another, and guess what? In the end, I win."

What if he breaks your heart?

"I will find another man, and another, if I have to. And in the end I win."

> *"A life lived on the sidelines is a life lost. The only way you win is to play, and to play with all you got. Give everything you have, leave nothing out on the field. Pass again after an interception, hand off after another fumble. Never stop stepping out, never quit putting it all on the line. If you do this, win or lose, in the end you WIN!"*
> —Scot Thomas Anderson

8. Face Your Fears.

"We gain strength, and courage, and confidence by each experience in which we really stop to look fear in the face...we must do that which we think we cannot."

—Eleanor Roosevelt

Use one through seven to get you ready, and now, let's face your fears. Not just face them, attack them.

I am afraid of heights, so what do I do? I charter a helicopter ride.

"Scot, you want the door on?"

"Nope. I will hang from the rails if you will let me. I guarantee I will get over this fear." I forced myself to look down the whole time. We landed that helicopter and I walked away saying, "I won. That is one fear out of my life."

You fear risk? Make yourself step out. You fear public speaking? Schedule yourself as many speaking engagements as you can in the next six months. Have the confidence in you to say, "You will lose, and I will win!"

Beat that thing that keeps stealing your reward!

System of Success (S.O.S.)
Excersise:

List your fears (from #1). Next list the consequences if you do not overcome the fear.

Fear:

Consequence:

How will I face and defeat that fear:

Fear:

Consequence:

How will I face and defeat that fear:

Fear:

Consequence:

How will I face and defeat that fear:

Fear:

Consequence:

How will I face and defeat that fear:

Fear:

Consequence:

How will I face and defeat that fear:

Fear:

Consequence:

How will I face and defeat that fear:

CHAPTER 19:

The Corridor Principle

*"I don't say these things because I believe in the
'brute' nature of man or that men must be brutalized to be
combative. I believe in God, and I believe in human
decency. But I firmly believe that any man's finest
hour—his greatest fulfillment to all he holds dear—
is that moment when he has to work his heart out in a
good cause and he's exhausted on the field of battle—
victorious."*
—Vince Lombardi

D r. Ronstadt a professor of entrepreneurship did a study
of the entrepreneurs going through the business program of the college. For twelve years, he studied these
young adults, trying to find the reason why some went out
and had a great deal of success (became very wealthy),
while others did not see that level of success, but instead,
just got a job and blended in with society.

He found out there was a difference between those
who were successful and made a lot of money and those
who did not. And it had nothing to do with their grades
in school, nothing to do with their I.Q., nothing to do with
their race or color, their past, their parents, or their upbring-

ing. The only difference he found was that the ones who were successful had the courage to launch businesses with no guarantee of success.

Dr Ronstadt came up with what he called "the corridor principle." He said:

> *"When you launch towards a goal, no matter the distance, you begin to move down a corridor of time. As you move, doors of opportunity will open that you would have never been able to see unless you had stepped out!"*
> —Dr Ronstadt

That one insight will change your life! As you begin to step out in life, with no guarantee of success, doors of opportunity begin to open up for you that you would have never seen had you not stepped out.

This is exactly how the wealthy do it. This is exactly why we don't. We sit around waiting for the doors to come to us, for opportunities to drop in our laps. You have been waiting fifteen years for the planets to all come into alignment so you could start your business. You've been waiting for the money, the people and the resources to drop in your lap. It never has happened and never will happen. But once you step out, the law of attraction attaches to your faith, which then brings the people, the resources and ideas you need to accomplish it. But you never would have gotten these things had you not stepped out.

This is the way we conduct our lives right now. When a door opens, I will go through it. When a business presents itself, I will do it! But there are no doors. The doors are down the hallway. YOU CANNOT SEE THE DOORS OF OPPORTUNITY UNTIL YOU STEP OUT! The doors will not come to you. You have to step towards them. It is time to get moving.

> **You cannot see the doors of opportunity until you step out!**

In 21 days, you will be stepping out, and when you do, you will see doors of opportunity that you never knew were available. The interesting thing is that they were always there. They were just up a little way, just a couple steps beyond what you could see.

You say, "You know, when I have money, I will invest."

No, no, no. To get lots of money, you will have to invest!

"When I have some security, I will take a risk."

But that's not a risk then.

"If I have a guaranteed business, then I'll do that."

No, no, no. That's not a risk! Without risk, there is no reward in your life. You have to step out in your life and then you will get.

Do you see how this works with expectation? I step out because I expect. If I didn't expect, I would not step out. My stepping out is in faith of what I expect. This activates the Law of Attraction, which then brings to me everything I need for success.

Let me give you an example in my own life. My father and I were walking around the mall one day with the wives. We were trying to come up with an innovative million dollar idea. We were brainstorming about fishing and golf. We had one idea after another until finally, we came up with a revolutionary putter, one that would change the industry.

Seven years ago, we would have talked about it for months, and then forgotten about it. And then ten years later, when it appeared on the market because someone else figured it out, we would have talked about how it was our idea.

Not anymore. Now we are risk takers. We step out. We decided we would throw $1,500 each at this thing and see what we could do with it. We made a list of what we had to do, and off we went.

Two days later, I was having lunch with a guy. I had no idea what he did. I started talking about the putter. He said, "I teach that type of engineering at the college. I will have some students work it out on the computer."

A few days later, he said the weirdest thing. "I met a guy who can make these. I can have him make us up a prototype for free."

Four days later, while talking to another guy, I find out he belongs to the PGA. He hooked us up with the *Golf Show*.

A few weeks later, Tiger Wood's childhood golf coach said he is interested in putting his name on the putter.

What happened was that we stepped out, and as we stepped down that corridor, our minds suddenly began to attract whatever we needed to have success. All these people had been there for years, but I would never have attracted them until I stepped out!

When I finally decided that I'm buying land, I didn't have the financing and I didn't have a lot of money in the bank. All I had was a realtor and good credit. I found some land and said, "I want it. Write a contract."

Two days later, a guy came into my life who got me zero down financing. A week later, a builder came across my path who could build for me for cheaper than anyone else. I found out a guy who had been my friend for years did architecture on the side and would do it for half price. I had been waiting for years to buy land, waiting for the financing, and the builder, the architect. Once I stepped out, all those doors became available to me.

> **Seven years ago, we would have talked about it for months, and then forgotten about it.**

One of my really good friends just five years ago was broke. I remember helping him move from his apartment, thinking, "Let's just burn all this junk rather than wasting time moving it." I thought of giving him $10 for all of it, just so we didn't have to move it.

Over the past five years, he has done the principles in this book. His first business had instant success for six months, but then the industry changed, and it tanked. I asked him what he was going to do.

He said, "I'm starting a magazine."

I said, "What do you know about that?"

He said, "Not much."

I said, "Who will write the articles?"

He said, "So far, just you—I hope."

I said, "Who will print it?"

He said, "Don't know."

"Do you have advertisers?"

He said, "Not yet. But in thirty days, we will have our first issue. I need my article from you by Friday."

He was laying it all on the line, every penny he had. He was stepping out into something that had no guarantee of success.

He stepped out and, boom, Robert Kiyosaki and his wife, the number one finance best-seller of this decade, did an article. Then John Maxwell signed up to do a monthly article. He got Miss America. He got two Phoenix Suns players and a PGA player. All this was in the first two months. His magazine instantly had enough advertisers. And in three months he is making, after paying all the bills, $40,000 plus a month.

All of that was right there all along, but he couldn't see it until he stepped out.

I wonder what is down your corridor. What million dollar ideas, companies, books, sales? What doors are waiting for you? You will never know until you step out!

CHAPTER 20:

Try, Try, Try, Try, Try— Oh, and Try Again

*"If I had my life to live over I'd like to make more
mistakes next time. I'd relax. I would limber up.
I would be sillier than I have been this trip.
I would take fewer things seriously. I would take more
chances. I would climb more mountains and swim more
rivers. I would eat more ice cream and less beans.
I would perhaps have more actual trouble, but I'd have
fewer imaginary ones. You see, I'm one of those people
who live sensibly and sanely hour after hour, day after
day. Oh, I've had my moments, and if I had to do it over
again, I'd have more of them. In fact, I'd try to have
nothing else. Just moments, one after another, instead of
living so many years ahead of each day. I've been one of
those persons who never goes anywhere without a
thermometer, a hot water bottle, a raincoat, and a para-
chute. If I had to do it again, I would travel lighter than
I have. If I had my life to live over, I would start barefoot
earlier in the spring and stay that way later in the fall.
I would go to more dances. I would ride more merry-go-
rounds, I would pick more daisies."*

—Nadine Stair

Law #11: The Law of Probability

The Law of Probability:
If you try something enough times, you will succeed.

If I hit enough golf balls, I will get a hole in one. It might take ten shots at it. It will probably take a few hundred thousand, but if I try enough times at something, I will succeed.

> *"Do the one thing you think you cannot do.*
> *Fail at it. Try again. Do better the second time.*
> *The only people who never tumble are those who*
> *never mount the high wire. This is your moment.*
> *Own it."*
> —Oprah Winfrey

How do we use this law in our favor? Well, if you start enough businesses, you will have a successful one. It may take three. It could take seven. Maybe ten. But if you try enough times, under the Law of Probability, you will succeed.

We hear that nine out of ten businesses fail, and we say, "I'm not going to try that. Those are some horrible odds."

A successful person says, "Do you mean I only have to start ten businesses to get a successful one? Those are some great odds." Once again, who cares that the first nine flopped? In the end, I win. With Business Ten, I made a million dollars.

Colonel Sanders retired at sixty-five. All he had was a fried chicken recipe that everyone said he should go into business with. He came up with a plan. He would give his recipe to a restaurant at no risk to them. All he wanted was a cut of the profits.

He went to his first restaurant. They said no. He went to a second. He went to his twenty-fifth. How many of us would have stopped at two? Maybe one? He went to his one hundredth. How many stop there? How about 500? How about 750? What about 1,000? I don't think I know a single person who would not quit after 1,000 rejections. That is a lot of outcomes (or failures, depending on your attitude).

> **If you try enough times, under the Law of Probability, you will succeed.**

On try number 1,007, he got a yes, and the rest is history. He used the Law of Probability. If I ask enough people, I know I will get a yes.

> *"Ever tried? Ever failed? No Matter, try again, fail again, Fail better."*
> —Samuel Beckett

This is my story of two friends. The names have been changed to protect the ugly. My two closest friends right out of high school, we will call Tim and Chuck.

Tim was one of the most handsome men you will come across—6'2", strong jaw, with that rugged manly look about him. If you asked any woman about him, she would say, "He is hot." Even though he is not 5'4" (who would have guessed).

Chuck, on the other hand (I will try to be nice about this), was pretty ugly. It looked like God was rushed, and he didn't have enough pieces to finish poor old Chuck. He looked like a big old weasel that was shoved onto a corndog stick.

Chuck and I were not too close in high school, yet I was amazed at how many hot girlfriends weasel boy got. Yet poor old Tim was trying to scrape together a date for prom. You will see that natural talent does not mean success. Risks mean success.

As a good Christian boy, this will trouble my mother to read. We had this dance place by Arizona State University (the Sundevils) called "The Devil House." It's just a dance place where I could go and meet the Proverbs 31 woman that God had for me. Of course I could never tell Momma I was going to the "Devil House," so I had to tell her we were going to a Christian Campus Bible Study. "Tonight, Mom, was awesome. We really dove into the book of Corinthians." (Sorry, Mom. It was done for the greater good.) The Devil House was wall-to-wall gorgeous women, and I am sure God would not want me not to go after the desires of my heart. It was truly the Promised Land flowing with silicone and honeys. (That is funny, but sorry, Mom, for writing that.)

Out of high school, Tim and I were best friends, so for the first four months, we went to Devil House together. Tim, the handsome one, and I would go in, pay our money, walk right by all the gorgeous women, making sure not to make eye contact. We would then walk right over to the pool tables and play pool for the rest of the night.

As the gorgeous girls walked by, we would talk about how next time we would ask them to dance. They passed by again, "Oh shoot, I missed her again. Next time I will ask her to dance." At the end of the night, we would be driving home, talking about all the girls we almost asked to dance. We talked about how next time we would get a dance. We did this nearly every weekend, most of the time Friday and Saturday nights, and then Sunday night for high school girl night.

> **I was amazed at how many hot girlfriends weasel boy got.**

Side note: How many of you sit around talking about the business you almost started, the invention idea you had that was put on the market by someone else, the land you almost bought and made a killing on?

Needless to say, I became an amazing pool player. Then one day Chuck and I started to hang out. One night Chuck said, "Let's go to the Devil House."

I said, "Sure." I loved to play pool.

Remember, Chuck is no Tim in the looks category. So we paid our money. I was headed for the pool tables. And all of a sudden, in front of me, Chuck walked right up to two gorgeous girls, both of whom were a foot taller than me, and asked them to dance. I almost wet my pants! Fear shot through my body. I started to tremble, and they looked at us like we were a dirty little piece of turd found on their shoes, chuckled at us and said in the meanest tone I have ever heard, "NO!"

I wanted to cry right there. I needed some counseling right that moment, because I had been emotionally wiped out. I grabbed Chuck and said, "What are you doing? We are supposed to play…"

Just then he grabbed two other gorgeous girls and said, "Would you like to dance?"

I let out a high pitched scream only dogs could hear. They said, "NO!"

In my sternest voice, I said, "Chuck, knock it off or I am going to kick your…"

"Hey, ladies, would you like to dance?"

They said, "No!"

I wanted to just crawl into the fetal position and suck my thumb. "Please, Jesus, come now," I begged. "I want the rapture. I'm out of here. I cannot take this pain."

Just then, I heard two girls say, "YES."

I said, "What?!"

"Yes, we would like to dance with you."

All of a sudden, all those nos meant nothing. I got a little rhythm moving up my leg, a little boogie in my soul. The next thing I knew, I was dancing, yes, dancing, with two of the hottest girls I had ever seen. I praised the Lord, telling Him, "You can take me now. I have lived life to its fullest."

The dance ended. I ran off that dance floor right up to the first two girls I saw. I said, "You want to dance?"

They said, "No."

I went to the next. They said, "No."

The next said, "No," but with the fourth, I heard once again those magic words, "Yes."

I screamed, "I knew it. If I ask enough girls to dance, there will be one that is desperate enough to dance with me.

For the next year, I went every weekend and I danced with hundreds of gorgeous women.

The Law of Probability was working in my life at age eighteen. It had nothing to do with talent or looks or a good upbringing. It had to do with risk.

Many of you are sitting in the pool table area of life, waiting for a hot deal to come find you. It ain't gonna happen. It is time you stepped out and said, "You want to dance? You want to dance? You want to dance?" If you try something enough times, I know you will succeed.

> **All of a sudden, all those nos meant nothing.**

I learned to look past the nos. Who cares about the five or six failures? It was the one amazing, awesome dance that made all the other failures go away. Remember, if you know in the end you get a dance, who cares about all the people who turn you down?

Every millionaire, every billionaire failed at businesses before they found the business that made them a million. You have to get it in your mind that if you try enough, you will be successful.

System of Success (S.O.S.)
Exercise

This is Scot Anderson's Dice Game of Probability: For this exercise you will need two dice.

There are over two million millionaires in America today. Over one million of those millionaires started out with less than one thousand dollars. One million of the self-made millionaires failed more than ten times in businesses. When they did finally start the right business, the average rate of their return was a hundred times. That's average. Some people made fifty times their investment. Some people made 200 times. Some made 500 times. The average rate of their return was 100.

What I want you to do is pick a number between 2 and 12. Write that below in the business column. Every turn, you will pick a number. You will do a little math here to keep track. Every number you pick represents a business that you start. You will start off with a thousand dollars. I don't care who you are. If you put your mind to it, you can come up with a thousand dollars to start a business.

In the investment column is how much you are going to invest. I have to let you know that there is a huge chance you will fail. The odds are greatly against you. You can, if you want, just hold onto your $1,000 and not risk losing it.

What you are going to do is roll both dice. If you do not roll your business, as you probably won't, you lose that $1,000. Each roll represents three months, so every three months, you can get a new $1,000. If you happen to hit on your business, you get 100 times the amount you invested.

Now go to the next line and write in your new investment. Once again you risk as much as you have. If you have zero, don't forget to get your new $1,000. But if you have $10,000, you can risk it all or part. See how long it takes you to become a millionaire.

Business (Your #)	Amount Invested	Number You Rolled	Made or Lost	Your New Total

Here is an example of one of my rounds in this game. It is not my best. In fact, it is closer to my worst. Realize that I have never not become a millionaire in this game.

First of all, I picked the number 7. Why? Seven has the best odds of coming up. Just like in business, you can start any business you want, but there are better businesses to start than others. There are businesses with better odds. Starting your own restaurant, you have a nine out of ten chance of failure. If you start a franchise restaurant, you have only a five out of ten chance of failure. The odds are better.

Forget that garbage about starting a business you love. Those business fail more than any others. You know what I love? Making money. Start a business that makes money. Once you have lots of money, start a business you love.

I risked all $1,000. It's like starting perhaps an eBay business, something cheap, inexpensive, with little start up cost. My first roll is a 6. I lost my money.

For the next three months, I reinvest another $1,000. Once again, I rolled a 6. I did this eight turns in a row. I rolled a number of 9s, a number of 4s. Do I quit, give up? I have invested all I have for three years. "Let's just stop. This will never work."

No risk, no reward. Finally, nine rolls and $9,000 later, a 7 comes up. That was nearly 3 years. But I hit $100,000.

I am going to now risk $10,000. I don't think it is wise to put all my eggs in one basket. So my next business venture might be writing a book. This might cost around

$10,000. Maybe I will buy some property with $10,000 down. This time it only took three rolls to hit a 7. I am now a millionaire.

Now let's invest $100,000. Let's start that dream restaurant. Six rolls later, I now have $10,000,000. It took me less than five years. It took some big risks. It took me sticking in there for nearly three years, failure after failure.

Do you see how the principles work with the Law of Probability? The whole purpose of that exercise is for you to be able to picture it. You start a business and in ninety days, it's not working? Either tweak it or scratch it and start another. It still didn't work? Do another. Finally, your business hits. Now do something bigger.

Chapter 21:

Sorry, I Don't Speak Wealthy

*"The beginning of knowledge is the discovery of
something we do not understand."*

—Frank Herbert

Law #12: The Law of Understanding

The Law of Understanding:
We only take action on those things that we understand.

When I say understand, I don't mean know. There
is a big difference between the two. You know
how to become wealthy. I have proved it throughout
this book. You know that you must take risks. You
know that you must invest. You have known this for
ten, twenty, thirty years. Knowing doesn't change a
thing. It is not until you understand it that you will take
action.

Nearly everyone knows how to have a great life, yet
few people experience it. Everyone pretty much knows
how to be successful yet few live it.

There are a lot of husbands who know how to be a
great husband. But they aren't.

We were out with a couple that I had been counseling with on their marriage. We went out and saw the movie *The Break Up*. All of the mistakes the man in the movie made, this guy was doing exactly the same things. After the movie, I wanted to see if he got it. I asked him about the movie. He said, "That guy was jerk. It would have been so simple for him to make it work."

"BINGO! It's the same for you." Of course, he never got it for himself. They ended up in divorce.

He knew how to be a good husband, but did not understand it. Had he understood it, he would have taken action. He would have changed.

The same is true for your life. Nothing will ever change until you understand the concept. Once you understand, you then can take action to change it.

A man goes to a marriage seminar and he hears how to treat his wife, but he doesn't understand it. If he understood it, he would step into a place where he was treating her like she was the most valuable thing in his life, taking her out, learning how to communicate with her, buying flowers and loving her unconditionally. But he goes home and does the same old things and wonders why he has the same old marriage. He heard but did not understand.

This is why you can go to a week-long seminar on investing, and one year later you still haven't invested. You know how, but you don't understand it.

Understanding is one of the most self-motivating forces in your life. Understanding is a producer. It always causes us to take action. When I understand something, it will change my life.

This final chapter is about teaching you how to get understanding in your life.

If a guy comes up to you and starts speaking a language you have never heard before, could you do what he was saying? No! You can't act if you don't understand. Let's say he speaks in French and you don't know French. Though you know the language is French, because you don't understand it, you can't take action. He might be screaming, "Fire, fire." To you, it means nothing.

> **Understanding is one of the most self-motivating forces in your life.**

"That is what learning is. You suddenly understand something you've understood all your life, but in a new way."
—Doris Lessing

The wealthy speak a different language than most of us reading this book. We hear them talking about investments, but it is French to us. We hear them talking about ways to make money, but they might as well be screaming, "Fire!" in French. It means nothing. You hear it. You know it, but you do not understand it.

"Listening to wealthy people talk, well it's all German to me!"
—Great Grandpa Anderson

My wife and I went to Europe for ten days. In France, pretty much everybody speaks French. My French is a little limited. I know "French fry," "French bread," "French poodle" and "French dressing." Oh, of course "we-we," but I think my translation is different then theirs. I found this out when I was trying to find a bathroom. So that is basically my French. After that, I am lost.

This limited me to a great degree in France. My lack of understanding limited my life. While walking down the street, hundreds of people were speaking French all around me. Somehow my mind blocked them out. But fifty yards away, I heard someone saying something in English. My ears instantly tuned in to hear what they were saying.

> *"Your mind will always block out that which it does not understand."*
> —Scot Thomas Anderson

It is interesting that your mind blocks out that which you do not understand. It is attracted by what you do understand. You may be hearing wealthy people talking all around you, talking about investment opportunities, but your mind blocks that out. You only speak just enough. So you don't hear the wealthy. But you can hear uncle Otto who doesn't have a dime to his name, talk about how now is not a good time to invest. You can hear him when he tells you not to start a business because it will fail. You then take action on what you understand.

Every restaurant we visited had the menu in French only, and a waiter whose English is about as broad as my French. If you know me at all, you know that eating is one of my favorite things to do. I love to eat, but in this love, I am a very picky eater. I know what I want, and I don't like to try anything new. Yes I do not take risks in my eating. Why try new when I know what I love? I am the type who loves food so much I will not risk a meal of having something I don't like just to try something new. It's not worth it to me.

> On these stupid French menus, the only thing I understood was spaghetti with Bologna.

On these stupid French menus, the only thing I understood was spaghetti with Bologna. So for every stupid meal, I just got spaghetti. After seven days, I would have sold my soul for a hamburger.

Now each menu contained a lot of different opportunities to have all the food my little heart desired, but the problem was that I do not understand the French language. I could not tap into the full potential. I was not limited by what I heard, because the waiter told me all the specials. I was limited by my understanding.

Throughout the different meals, I would see something go by and say, "I should have gotten that. I wonder what that is."

How many times in life did we say, "I should have done that invention. I should have ordered that business." Why didn't we? Because we did not understand.

In the menu of life, we have the opportunity to order all we desire. We have the opportunity to order the abundance, but since we don't have the understanding, we continue to order the spaghetti of life and we continue to stay right in the exact same place. We are sick of the spaghetti of life, but we don't want to risk getting something we don't like.

In your life, how many times have you said, "I should have bought that land?" Seven years ago, you drove by land and said, "I should have bought that last year. I would have made a bundle." Five years ago you drove by that land and said, "I should have bought that land. I would have made a bundle." Three years ago or last week. It's the same thing. When do you say, "Hey! If I buy that land today, in two years, I can make a bundle."? When do you finally understand?

How many invention ideas have you had? "Man, I had that idea. I should be the millionaire." The reason you're not is because you don't speak the language. You don't understand. So you never step out.

You hear so many opportunities, but until you learn the language and start to understand it, you will never step out into the abundance.

In the late 80s, I had one of my college teachers say, "Buy Microsoft."

I said, "I am only making $3.35 an hour."

He said, "Take whatever you can and buy it."

I don't think anyone in the class took notice of that. If I had bought at ten, twenty dollars a week, I would have two million dollars in stock. I heard but did not understand.

We look at most of the wealthy people out there and we think they made most of their money on land. "Man, are they lucky." Did you see that? It never clicks. We never look at the light bulb and say, "Maybe I should look into that."

If I wanted to learn French, what would I have to do? I would have to get books, CDs and maybe get a tutor (seminars). I would have to study it. It would take me hundreds and hundreds of hours. Finally one day, while walking down the street, someone says something in French and my mind says, "Hey, we understand that." Finally I can take action.

> Until you learn the language and start to understand it, you will never step out into the abundance.

Understanding comes by hearing and hearing and hearing, by studying, and studying.

When I first decided I was sick of just getting by and I wanted to be one of the wealthy, the first thing I did was to find out what the wealthy did to get where they are. I asked a wealthy mentor what I should do.

He said, "The most important thing you can do is invest."

I said, "Cool. Invest in what?"

He said, "The most important investment you will ever make is to invest in yourself."

I said, "What do you mean?"

He said, "How many books on wealth have you read in the last year?"

I said, "Almost two."

He said, "There is your problem. The average millionaire reads two a week."

The average millionaire got to where he is today because when he was where you are today, he invested $200 or more a month into himself—buying books, tapes, and going to seminars.

I went out and bought thirty books and 300 hours of CDs. I then began to read and read and read. I listened to CDs everywhere I went. Months went by, but nothing had changed yet.

Finally, I decided to look at some property (action). We were looking at a particular lot and I asked the realtor how much it was.

He said, "$225,000."

I said, "You mean pesos right? Because two years ago, I could buy this thing for $100,000." I said, "No thanks."

As I was getting in the car, it clicked. All of sudden, all that information I had been studying, all those CDs took hold. All of a sudden, I started understanding the language of the wealthy.

Rather than seeing how much I lost, I saw how much this other person gained. If I bought it today, how much would it be worth next year. I said, "Let's buy it." Two months later I sold it for $300,000. And that catapulted me into where I am today.

I started to understand the language. Once I understood it, I could take action.

The wealthy speak a different language. We speak the language of just enough. We speak the language of average.

Where did we learn it? Where did you learn to speak English? Usually from those who raised you. If your parents spoke the language of "just enough," that is what you speak today. You grew up learning to just get a job and get by, to avoid taking risks. Just work your job.

It is time we begin to speak the language of too much, the language of living a destiny and a dream. It is time we learn the language so we can begin to order all of our hopes and dreams from the menu of life.

I challenge you to do what I did. Invest in the greatest investment opportunity you have—YOU! Do what I did. Cut out cable TV, high speed Internet and fast food. I then spent $200 a month on me, on books and tapes and seminars. We must learn to speak a different language. We have to understand it if we ever want to take action in our lives.

EPILOGUE

As of right now, you are just 21 days from being a millionaire on the inside. I challenge you to apply every one of the laws to your life.

- Become responsible for your life. In this you will be in control of your life.

- Remember you are happy to the degree to which you are in control. Control those thoughts. Every thought is a seed that will produce. Will you be producing out of your faith or out of your fears? You choose.

- Grab those reins of thought, and make them go towards your dreams and desires.

- Always substitute the positive for the negative. We allow no limiting thought into our minds.

- Remind yourself of who you are becoming. Remember, the clearer the vision you have of yourself, the faster you will get there.

- Work on that self-esteem. "I love myself." You are the greatest you ever created, don't forget it.

- Change your attitude by changing what you expect. Tomorrow will be a great day. Today is a great day. Every day is full of opportunities, opportunities that will take me to my dreams. Circumstances do not dictate how I feel. I choose how I feel. I am responsible for my attitude! What is amazing is, I will get exactly what I expect out of life!

- I am a risk taker. Without risks, there are no rewards. Using the Law of Attraction as I step out, I step down the corridor of success, and doors of opportunities present themselves, doors I would have never seen had I not stepped out. Using the Law of Attraction, what I expect and step out into, I attract the people, the ideas, and the resources I need to accomplish.

- In the end I win, so there is nothing to be afraid of. There are no failures, only results. I learn and grow from each result. It may take me ten business, but the one successful business makes me forget all about the other nine.

- Become committed to growing and changing. Read two books a week. Turn off that stupid radio, and listen to self-help CDs. Turn of the constant negative news CNN, and turn on something that will take you towards your ideal self.

I challenge you to read this book again and again. Keep reading it until you understand it. How do you know when you understand something? You begin to take action. When your life starts to change, that is when you know you understand it.

Thank you so much for allowing me to speak into your life. May you be blessed in all that you do. May you live a long, happy, prosperous life, surrounded by those you love. Please remember that relationships are the most important thing. You were created for relationships, and until you are developing, maintaining, and experiencing them in the right way, you will live your life below the level in which you were created to live.

Like my wife says, live, laugh, and love. Isn't that what life is all about?

Featured Products for Scot Anderson

Think Like a Billionaire, Become a Billionaire

Dad

Mom

More Than A Dad

Millionaire Habits in 21 Days

To order or for more information,
visit Life House Books online at:

www.lifehousebooks.com

Life House
BOOKS

WOULD YOU LIKE TO HAVE SCOT SPEAK AT YOUR CONFERENCE, CHURCH, SCHOOL...?

S cot will carefully customize his talk for you and your audience. Contact us today for full information on booking Scot to speak at your next meeting or conference. Visit millionairehabitsin21days.com or write to Scot Anderson, 3520 East Brown Road, Mesa, Arizona 85213.